FORGOTTEN LEADERS

Guiding America's Veterans from
Soldier to Student to Success!

FORGOTTEN LEADERS

Guiding America's Veterans from
Soldier to Student to Success!

DANIEL BOLAN

DEFIANCE PRESS
& PUBLISHING

Forgotten Leaders: Guiding America's Veterans from Soldier to Student to Success!

ISBN-13: 978-1-948035-48-4 (Paperback)
ISBN-13: 978-1-948035-49-1 (ebook)

Edited by Janet Musick
Cover designed by Spomenka Bojanic
Interior designed by Debbi Stocco

Published by Defiance Press and Publishing, LLC

Bulk orders of this book may be obtained by contacting Defiance Press and Publishing, LLC. www.defiancepress.com.

Public Relations Dept. – Defiance Press & Publishing, LLC
281-581-9300
pr@defiancepress.com

Defiance Press & Publishing, LLC
281-581-9300
info@defiancepress.com

TABLE OF CONTENTS

FOREWORD..9

INTRODUCTION—THE SVF MISSION 13
A Group too Essential to be Forgotten.................................13
The Mission of SVF..14
The Mission of this Book...15

CHAPTER 1—EXPLORING THE PROBLEM............................17
Politics, Military Leadership & Civilian Action 17
The Big Picture 18
Student Life: What Veterans Really Go Through 19
Graduation Rates & Career Placement 23
My Beliefs About Honor..24

CHAPTER 2—BOTH MONEY & TALENT ARE BEING WASTED 25
Service & Sacrifice Should be Rewarded, Not Wasted..........25
Where Does the Money Go? 27
Where Does the Talent Go?..30

CHAPTER 3—CAMPUSES NEED STUDENTS TO LEAD EACH OTHER ..33
Large Universities Need Leadership......................................33
Student Veterans in Student Government 36
The Value of Leadership 37

CHAPTER 4—VETS BECOME ISOLATED................................39
Veterans Disconnected from Other Students 40
Dealing with Civilian Peers..40
Connecting with Other Student Veterans 41
Student Veterans Disconnected from Faculty 42
Discussing Politics with Others on Campus 43

CHAPTER 5—PROBLEMS WITH CURRENT RESOURCES....................47
Are There Current Student Veterans Groups?.....................47
What Services Should Look Like 48

CHAPTER 6—STORIES FROM VETERANS 53
Interview with Michael Cullen 54
Personal History 54

Lessons & Impacts 57
Advice & Looking Forward 58
Interview with Sheriff Payton Grinnell.................................... 60
Personal History 60
Lessons & Impacts 63
Advice & Looking Forward 64
Interview with Mark Singleton 66
Personal Story.. 66
Lessons & Impact.. 69
Advice & Looking Forward 71

CHAPTER 7—TAPPING INTO THE UNTAPPED RESOURCES.............. 73
Helping Vets Navigate College Easily 73
Recognizing Veterans' Leadership.. 74
The Financial Assistance & Guidance Veterans Deserve 75
Long-Term Effects 77

CHAPTER 8—REVERSING THE ISOLATION THAT VETS FEEL............ 79
Building Veterans' Hopes & Dreams 80
Connection with Job Potential 82

CHAPTER 9—THE SVF COMMUNITY 85
Student Veteran Academic Support.. 86
Servant Leadership in Working with Veterans........................ 87
Student Veterans' Sports Groups.. 88
A Shared Vision 89

CHAPTER 10—WITH HONOR AND GRATITUDE 91
Who is Daniel Bolan? 91
Student Veterans Foundation is Something Different 92
The Message of SVF 94

CHAPTER 11—MAXIMUM MEMORY MASTERY 95

CHAPTER 12—WHAT IS THE CURRICULUM? WHERE DO WE
START?.. 103
Mind Mapping.. 103
Finding Your Learning Buddies/Team 104
The Most Frequently Asked Question 105
What Are Tips for Memory and Creativity? 106
What Else Is in M3?.. 107
What Comes Next? 108
What Is the Leadership Frameworks Course? 109
What Is GIGG? 110

Table of Contents

What Else Is in Frameworks? 111
Netting Out Leadership Frameworks 112
Background to this Course 112
Leaving IBM And Founding Dottino Consulting Group 113
The Elements of GRI 113
Who Is This for? 114

CONCLUSION 117
Share Our Message 117

ENDNOTES AND REFERENCES 119

FOREWORD

Rarely in life do we get to meet an individual as accomplished in life or as dedicated to a noble life's ambition as Daniel Bolan. What's even rarer is the fact that Daniel is only 21 years old. He's an Eagle Scout, state champion bowler, patriot and a leading advocate for our men and women in uniform.

Probably more amazing than his accomplishments so far in his young life to date is the fact that Daniel has the vision and the insight to recognize a significant gap in how America supports her military heroes. As many veterans leave the military and return home, they are not necessarily prepared to deal with the transition back to a student and all that transition entails. The G.I. Bill is available to veterans, but the fact is that the G.I. Bill does not cover all expenses. Also, the returning veteran must navigate the paperwork involved, adapt to a college social environment that is starkly different than military life, and continue to support themselves and their families.

Daniel founded the Student Veterans Foundation (SVF) for the sole purpose of providing the sorely needed support and resources needed by veterans returning to finish their education after defending our freedom throughout the world. These veterans are returning to an environment where the demographics are wildly different from what they're used to, where the average age of their student colleagues is much younger, where most are still single, and where there is very little structure. Add to these facts that on-campus resources for the veterans who may be dealing with their own set of issues, such as the stress of young married life or even post-traumatic stress syndrome, and you have some very unique challenges that most in the traditional student body are not facing.

Many veterans, who faced life-and-death decisions almost on a daily basis in combat situations may find the process of finding a like-minded study group mostly impossible. A significant percentage of both part-time and full-time student veterans drop out. Sadly, student veterans have lower graduation rates than traditional college students.

At his core, Daniel believes the service and sacrifice of these veterans should be rewarded and celebrated, not wasted. He also believes the incredible talent pool that exists with these returning veterans is being under-utilized, largely due to the lack of support for those returning to further their education.

Daniel adroitly points out the shortcomings of the existing support mechanisms for these student veterans, with solid recommendations on how to improve the access and delivery of the tools necessary to capitalize on their immense talent.

Daniel's recommendations should be embraced by all institutions of higher learning, openly acknowledging the incredible value the student veteran brings to campus, their fellow students, and America as a whole. His vision, which is beyond his years, should be one shared by all Americans.

As President John F. Kennedy, referring to our veterans, once said, "As we express our gratitude, we must never forget that the highest appreciation is not to utter words, but to live by them."

Daniel Bolan's actions proves he hasn't forgotten; he has dedicated his life to the appreciation of these returning veterans and all Americans should support his cause.

– David Thomas Roberts

Introduction—The SVF mission

Remember the last time you experienced something life-changing? Remember how it felt like the ground had crumbled under your feet and, although you weren't sure how to move forward, the whole world kept going? The one thing that's constant in life is change, and the only thing a person can do is learn to navigate those changes.

Changes present us with opportunities, with the chance to do something differently, but it's impossible to do something in a new way if all you have are old tools. In addition to that, if your mind has been changed by recent experience, you need more than updated tools—you need the kind of support that comes from shared experience. You need a community and a higher power to turn to. God calls each of us to lift each other up and, when we see a person going through change, a person who needs help, we must do all we can.

A Group too Essential to be Forgotten

There is a serious problem today on our college and university campuses: hundreds of thousands of students are not receiving the resources they need to be successful. Although they may not be stressed about the cost of higher education like so many of their peers, they are stressed by factors that are invisible to others around them. Other students, their teachers, the administration—the people who share their day-to-day college-lives do not share their daily experiences. Although they are surrounded, they often become lost and lonely in the middle of this crowd.

I am speaking of our student veterans. Those brave men and women who have dedicated time, sacrificed their safety, and endured the pressures of military life. These soldiers, sailors, Marines, and airmen and women return to civilian life, burdened with their experiences and struggling with major life transitions. Many of them choose to pursue college educations, whether for the first time or as a continuation of what they were doing before their enlistment. And these student veterans, a precious resource to the future of our country, do not receive just service for their sacrifice.

This problem costs our country dearly, it costs civilians and taxpayers dearly and, most of all, it costs these courageous men and women dearly.

I see the costs to this country accumulating, and I feel passionate about helping others. For many years, I have dedicated my time to leading my peers through serving the veterans in my community and across the country. And the problems that our student veterans face are so prevalent to me that I simply cannot sit by and watch. I must act.

THE MISSION OF SVF

My name is Daniel Bolan, and I am a young man from Central Florida. I am not the central figure in this story but, if you know anything about me, you should know that I admire people who exhibit *greatness*. Excellence is rare and, when I see it, I want to be a part of it; I want it to spread.

As a child, I looked up to my grandfathers, admiring them for their service in the U.S. Army. One grandfather, Joe Bolan, served during World War II, and the other, Lee Kitchens, served during the Korea Conflict. I always looked up to them. As a teenager, I was blessed with many gifts, including excellent hand-eye co-ordination, which contributed to me becoming a champion bowler and a member of international teams. As an athlete, I was often approached by organizations looking for sponsorship and endorsements but, based on my father's advice, I waited until I could partner with exactly the right program. After appearing in several charity competitions as a representative of various veterans' associations and veterans' groups, I decided that the best way I could handle my representation of veterans was to become the founder of my own organization. With the help of my dedicated, visionary father Chris Bolan, the Strike for Vets organization was born.

After five years of public appearances and winning championships on behalf of the inspirational veterans in my life and the wounded warriors I have known over the years, Strike for Vets is growing. Since 2018, it has come under the wing of the Student Veterans Foundation (SVF), as part of the SVF live events initiative and, in 2019, we expanded from being an organization only represented in professional bowling to an organization represented in baseball and softball as well. I am proud to be the founder of SVF and to expand my goals to assist veterans in every way possible.

But it doesn't stop here. It only begins now, with you.

THE MISSION OF THIS BOOK

This book, *Forgotten Leaders*, is my collection of thoughts regarding the mission, the purpose, and the goals of SVF. While I want SVF to take immediate, effective action, our initial growth means less than long-term results. The performance of the book's mission will ultimately be judged by the success of the SVF mission, not by this book itself, but I am hoping to reach as many veterans and veteran supporters as possible. I feel that explaining my research, my point of view, and my dream for helping all student veterans is the sure way to reach many veterans, their families and their friends, in many communities. Based on my travels around the country, the conversations I've had with veterans of all ages, and the research compiled in these pages, I believe that veterans, and those who love them, want to know these things, even if they aren't aware of it yet.

I have collected the most valuable of what I've found into a single place, and I hope to explore not only the need for change, but to show you the path I propose that will get us to our end goal: tangible impacts in the lives of veterans. Changing the systems may not be easy, but if it achieves results for the men and women who have fought for my freedom, then not a single struggle that I have endured was in vain.

You will find resources and references for veterans throughout the book, as well as a detailed collection of them at the end. Please explore them, reach out, and share them with every veteran you know.

This book is designed to provide student veterans with information they can use to succeed in school and in the civilian workforce. It is designed to explain why it's important to support our veterans on college campuses, and it is designed to explain my vision for how to best support them.

I know my vision may be incomplete. SVF and the list of services we want to provide is always growing. If you feel I've left out any important elements, or if you have ideas for how to connect and help veterans in your community, please contact me via the SVF website. Let's work together to expand the resources that keep veterans engaged, fully utilized, and remembered as a vital part of our American community.

http://studentveteransfoundation.org/

Chapter 1—Exploring the Problem

Politics, Military Leadership & Civilian Action

I find it interesting that, throughout U.S. history, the majority of presidents served in the military. Nearly all branches are represented—the Army, Navy, reserve forces and National Guard. The leader of the country, the commander-in-chief of the national military, has often had direct, personal military experience.

In the past 75 years, the pattern has shifted, so that there is now a long gap in the history of presidents with military experience. The most recent president with a military record was George W. Bush, who served from 1968-1974, some thirty years before he took office at the White House. That means that, today, no president has served in the military in nearly 50 years.[1]

This seems to be one example of the disconnect I see between political leadership and political rhetoric—while many politicians and their institutions claim that they are supportive of the military and the needs of its service members, they have no direct experience leading those service members. Until they step into the highest office in the country, that is.

The best presidents have chosen to keep the top-ranked leaders of our military close to them as advisors and cabinet members, pulling close to themselves the needs of this vital population of our country. As long as the political leadership is aligned with the military leadership, the government is doing what it can to keep the needs of military service members top of mind.

It is then up to the civilians to support that vital partnership. As a student, a tax payer, and an admirer of veterans I've known who have personally affected me, I see it as part of my personal duty and mission to support the partnership between as many people as possible, in support of the men and women who fight daily for my freedom.

THE BIG PICTURE

I became aware of how many service men and women are discharged from the military every year: nearly 3.3 million in 2017.[2] Every month, tens of thousands of people join the U.S. workforce, well-trained adults with worldly experience. Additionally, more than 10% of those have likely deployed overseas in the past year, and 25% of them have been overseas in the past two years.[3]

I began to wonder: *How many of these men and women have been in combat situations? How do they acclimate to civilian life? What do they do when they return?*

I then learned that nearly 1 million veterans are enrolled in our higher education[4] systems every year. I learned how low their graduation rates are; I learned how much they struggle to get their degree so they can get good jobs to support their families and themselves. Then, I learned how the services available to them are limited and mainly focused on employment transition; the services are also struggling, so they aren't able to provide the proper support these soldiers deserve.

I learned how veterans who choose to return to school are supported financially by the G.I. Bill, but that the educational expenses covered are minimal.[5] [6] I was shocked to discover how G.I. Bill monies have been involved in numerous scandals[7] in recent decades, and that our veterans are not being properly informed on how the G.I. Bill works and how it can benefit them. This valuable resource, this life-changing assistance, can be much better used if only the veterans receive the help they need.

I feel this is no small issue. It is an expensive issue—both financially and emotionally. It is a moral issue. It is imperative that I help address this.

STUDENT LIFE: WHAT VETERANS REALLY GO THROUGH

According to my research, student veterans are facing struggles that traditional students do not face. While they may receive the financial support of the G.I. Bill, they often face financial obligations from their active duty life, including a mortgage or family responsibilities. One JAG officer I spoke with indicated that, if these student veterans don't have a good support officer, they can run through their G.I. money quickly. I spoke with a head recruiter at a state National Guard, and he affirmed that he struggles with the same situation.

Is providing them with the money to pay for tuition and fees truly enough for them to be successful in college? Is it truly enough for them to enjoy college worry-free or, at least, for them to minimize their stress about personal finances so they can focus on their studies?

Let's break down some recent information about student veteran enrollment:

✓ Approximately 75% of student veterans are male and 25% are female.[8]

✓ The age range of student veterans with the highest percentage is 24 to 40 years old.[9]

✓ Nearly half of all student veterans have children.[10]

✓ About half of all student veterans are married.[11]

✓ Nearly two-thirds of student veterans are first-generation college students.[12]

✓ 80% of student veterans are enrolled in public colleges, the remaining 20% is split between private and for-profit universities.[13]

What does this mean, if we look at the average student veteran on our college campuses?

✓ It means that male veterans go from a structured military environment, made up of roughly 17% women,[14] to a college campus, where roughly 56%[15] of the population is female. While, of course, these men have likely grown up in educational environments that included females, a college campus is a much different environment than a high school campus, requiring different social skills to navigate. And their recent experience of four years or more in a male-dominated environment is a large cultural difference from most college campuses. Female student veterans may also find that the mentality, attitudes, and social conventions of their classmates at a university are shockingly different from the male-dominated attitudes and policies of military life.

✓ It means that the student veteran is roughly between 5 and 22 years older than his or her classmates. Imagine yourself surrounded by people 15 years younger than you or 15 years older than you, and how much extra effort it requires to connect with those people than it does to connect with people who are closer to your age.

✓ It means that nearly all the student veterans on campus have family responsibilities—duties to a spouse or children—that may take priority over social gatherings, casual study-groups, or even schoolwork. It means that in order to support these families, many veterans are juggling full- or part-time employment while enrolled in classes. It means that parental concerns, such as finding reliable childcare, are part of the daily list of responsibilities, which can be very different realities and concerns from traditional students.

✓ It means that two-thirds of student veterans cannot rely on members of their family for the kind of emotional or psychological support that many other students can. When a student is the first person in their family to attend college, they may not have anyone to turn to for advice, guidance, or to discuss the burdens and pressures of school. Their family may not understand what they're doing, what they're studying, or how much time college work actually takes. They may have to reschedule or miss family gatherings because of school responsibilities, and their families may see this as offensive or give the veteran grief for not showing familial love, simply because they don't understand the veteran's situation.

✓ It means that nearly 80% of student veterans go from a structured, highly regulated environment to a general student pool where everyone is swimming in their own direction.[16] In addition, there are specific processes and bureaucratic steps to follow at every university, and no clear direction where to find answers. Students may get shuffled back and forth to multiple departments in order to complete registration and financial aid paperwork, and they won't know if it isn't done correctly until a piece of mail, which includes a bill and additional fees, arrives. The 20% of student veterans who attend private and for-profit schools are burdened with additional financial costs, not to mention potential cutthroat environments associated with advanced professional fields (such as law or medicine) or competitive trade professionals (such as auto-mechanics or cosmetology).[17] [18]

This is my interpretation of the facts based on the veterans I've spoken with, but there's more hard numbers that support my argument that veterans are obviously struggling. Student veterans experience higher rates of high-risk behaviors like substance abuse, as well as psychological disorders, such as post-traumatic stress disorder (PTSD) and depression.[19] Student veterans report feeling "bored" with college life. After traveling the world and being involved in the action and camaraderie of the military, they miss the connection that comes through shared experiences. They also feel like their peers are "immature" and can often feel like their perspectives as military service members are unwelcome in classroom discussion.

Many of these student veterans are carrying heavy emotional burdens that they have difficulty relating to other students.[20] They may need help reorienting themselves to civilian life after what they have lived through, especially if they were deployed to combat zones or saw multiple incidents of military action, whether it was direct engagement in combat or not. They begin to feel isolated and disconnected from the people around them, which can distract them from learning or impede their ability to learn the class materials presented to them.

Many veterans require additional medical services to help them deal with PTSD, depression, anxiety, or a number of physical health issues. While many universities have pharmacies and medical services on campus, only some accept military health insurance, and many other campuses don't offer those services at all. Having to travel off-campus for medical services can make setting medical or therapy appointments difficult for many student veterans. Unlike many of their fellow students, veterans aren't able to take full advantage of the university campus services, although they must still pay the full amount of fees.[21]

Because of age, lifestyle, employment, and cultural differences between military life and university life, these veterans might struggle their entire time as a student, or it could mean they never even finish.

While we attempt to take the financial burden off our student veterans by supplying them with the G.I. Bill and helping them become enrolled in college, they need far more than that to succeed. Specifically, they need financial guidance and even access to affordable veterans' benefits lawyers to help coach them through the financial issues they face while in school. Throwing money at their education simply isn't enough, and it's in the best interest of all Americans to help them.

GRADUATION RATES & CAREER PLACEMENT

Although student veterans have already proven their potential with their service, the disconnect and isolation they feel on college campuses, combined with additional financial and family responsibilities, can work against them, contributing to failure. Lower graduation rates of student veterans are ultimately an inefficient use of G.I. Bill monies, costing the American taxpayer innumerable dollars every year.

One survey found that 37% of part-time and 16% of full-time veterans dropped out of college within nine months—or in just two semesters, on average. It varies at different types of schools, but the overall graduation rates for veterans are lower than the rates for nonveterans.[22]

Student veterans have the potential to be some of the highest performing of all college students. They flourish under routine, thrive with a sense of direction and purpose, and may take deadlines very seriously. It's common for a veteran who didn't perform all that well in high school to return to college with a renewed sense of dedication and focus, then average a GPA of 3.5 or higher during their studies.[23]

Yet, it is an uphill struggle for them the entire time, depending whether they can connect with other students enough to form study groups and supportive on-campus relationships. Without this vital support, student veterans can experience more difficulty in completing their coursework.

MY BELIEFS ABOUT HONOR

I have been raised to believe in honor. I believe in paying respect for people who show they deserve it, and I believe in making your dreams into reality. The American Dream is a part of my everyday life, and I genuinely believe that this is the home of the free *because* of the brave. That speaks volumes to those who understand it.

I believe that no one's past dictates his or her future. I believe that mistakes can be remedied and no longer need to control what you can do, or what you actually accomplish. Problems don't prevent solutions, and tomorrow remains more important than yesterday, because it stays ahead of you. It's the first day of the rest of your life, so start living for tomorrow, today.

It's an honor to serve this country, and there's honor in serving. Veterans step forward to lead from the front, to serve the rest of their country, and we should acknowledge and support their sacrifice. It's important to honor those who have served because, without them, we wouldn't be living in the country that values freedom and liberty. We don't send these men and women out into battle alone, and we can't send them into the battlefield of life after service alone either.

Chapter 2—Both Money & Talent Are Being Wasted

Service & Sacrifice Should be Rewarded, Not Wasted

When the U.S. did away with the draft and instituted an all-volunteer military, it changed the course of both American and world history. U.S. service members *choose* to participate in military service—they are not compelled to it by law or any other outside force—and the reasons they choose to serve vary with each individual. However, there are common themes regarding the superior opportunities that a military life can offer.

Compared with many other militaries in the world, the U.S. military offers excellent lifelong benefits, including a reasonable and fair salary, educational opportunities (both in the military as well as after, with the G.I. Bill), and a lifelong health insurance option, in addition to many discounts and special organization memberships. Many American business owners offer incentives for their customers who served. These reasons make military enlistment a coveted position rather than a standardized one—military service truly sets individuals apart from their peers, and every American knows that a military uniform symbolizes *sacrifice*, not *obligation*.

Compared with compulsory militaries, American service members are better educated and prepared for military life. Before applying for military service, all service members have to complete a high school education. While it may sound basic, this standard is not even required in many countries and is something distinct that gives our military an edge immediately. In addition to their basic high school education and basic training, all service members receive advanced training in one field or another, making them a critical part of the military machine.

Compared with many other countries' militaries, U.S. service members are provided with unique opportunities to live abroad, either on deployment or in a long-term assignment. The U.S. has an active military presence in dozens of countries around the world and, depending on the specifics of a service member's training, he or she may be assigned to be stationed in a foreign nation. Many people consider this a particularly enticing reason to join the military, as well as an invaluable part of their military experience. One veteran I spoke with who grew up in Michigan stated that it was only because of the military that he was able to see the ocean. If it hadn't been for the Marine Corps, he never would have had the opportunity to live in Okinawa, Japan, or visit Germany, Thailand, or Australia. He told me that no one he went to high school with has any similar experiences, as most of them never even left the state. The international travel and experience of life abroad greatly affects every member who is assigned to serve in another nation, whether or not they were exposed to international travel before their enlistment.

Service members are counting on their military experience to pay off once their enlistment is over. They have received training, and they have learned to do many valuable things and, when preparing to transition to civilian life, they know they must rely on their grit and the problem-solving skills they learned in the military to get them through to a long-term career.

While the American public has already invested in these individuals' basic education and life-changing experiences, when they choose to turn around and serve that same civilian public after military enlistment, the advanced training and valuable international travels they experienced in the military can ultimately go to waste. Once they leave the environment, if the civilian public doesn't immediately see a use for a soldier's training or experience, or if the veteran doesn't immediately find a way to monetize his or her military life, the millions of dollars spent on educating that service member will just get thrown away.

Where Does the Money Go?

It all starts with recruiting new service members. This is a process of advertising, creating interest, and even investing in some college or enlistment bonuses at the beginning of the service member's career. Then, new recruits need to be paid and provided with health insurance benefits and medical services; they are provided moving, housing and storage expenses; they are provided uniforms and regulation gear. Once a service member begins training, let's also factor in the cost of the salaries of those higher-ranking officers and enlisted members who will train them.

On average, these costs add up to just under $45,000 per new Marine, for the first year of enlistment, according to one 2017 study. You read that right—it costs approximately $45,000 to get a Marine through the first year of enlistment.

In addition to that, an officer in training can choose to go to college in the first years of enlistment and attain training in highly specialized or advanced fields. For an officer who is working on an engineering or another highly technical college degree, the cost for four years of college can be as much as $340,000, or more.

Also, in his or her first year, the Marine will receive various equipment and procedural training and, while the Marine is beginning to work off some of the costs they have already accumulated, these months of training are also associated with invisible expenses. General training equipment and training facilities, as well as individual equipment assigned to each Marine, has its own cost, and that doesn't touch the cost of satellites, drones, or fighter jets.[24]

The standard in the military is to make sure that each soldier is a leader and has at his or her disposal the basic skills to save themselves and their fellow soldiers if technological assistance isn't available. Each soldier is taught basic first aid, weapon maintenance, cooking skills, and even soft skills, including team-building and communication methods. On the other hand, training never stops at basic skills, and U.S. soldiers are given more access to high-tech training than any other military in the world. For example, a soldier will be trained in the basic skills of navigating using a paper map and compass and, once that level is achieved, he or she will be trained on GPS and mobile device technologies.[25]

Lastly, any time a service member is deployed to a combat zone, they may receive specialized gear and equipment that had not been assigned to them before, so let's factor in the costs of combat equipment in our evaluation.

What does it cost to fully equip a Marine for battle? According to one journalist's research, it costs about $5,000 for a full uniform, rifle, equipment, fully packed rucksack, and daily pay and meals. And each soldier must be fully trained on how to use that rifle, the equipment, and his or her body and mind when engaged in active combat. This type of training is crucial—non-negotiable—and is often invisible, although it is really "standard issue."[26] With as many as 100,000 active duty U.S. soldiers deployed in various stations around the world on any given day, this cost is no small burden for taxpayers to bear. Of course, this cost is not where the majority of training expense comes in.

When we focus specifically on the cost of the training our military service members receive, it's difficult to calculate exact numbers.[27] In addition to the salaries of training officers and the cost of training equipment, the U.S. military has some of the best training facilities in the world, capable of immersing soldiers in virtual or full-scale training scenarios, which better prepares them for real-world situations. And, of course, there are the costs of transporting service members from one base to another, one assignment to the next, and to the specific training facility where the training is provided. Some of the time, service members themselves must bear some of the cost burdens of transportation, depending on the situation but, often, it is a part of our military budget to account for moving troops to a location for necessary training.

One analysis indicates that the average annual cost to train an average soldier is $17,000.[28] Of course, it depends on what the service member is doing and how extensive the training needed. For example, it is more costly to train pilots, medical personnel, and submarine engineers than it is to train building maintenance or automotive technicians. But, ultimately, we are talking about many millions of dollars in training that are spent annually on making sure our active duty soldiers know how to do their jobs.

Do we want to throw that away when these veterans leave the military? They have been working hard to master the skills the military required of them, displaying excellence in order to be efficient and reliable when called upon. How can we civilians not value and want to maintain that sense of duty? Do we really care about our future? Because, if we do, we will figure out a way to stop all that money from blowing away like dust in the wind. Our military is the best and most well-trained in the world, and there are good reasons for that.

Before you start to wonder whether these costs are worth it in the long run, consider the advanced state of the U.S. military. We have set the precedent as one of the leaders of technology in the past half-century, as well as have created a humane and rights-forward environment for our service members, unlike many militaries throughout the world. My point is not that the costs are too high, it is that the value Americans extract from them is too low. Veterans know how to effectively perform more skills than general society knows how to use and, so, much of the valuable training the military provides, which currently goes to waste, could be much more valuable if harnessed.

Where Does the Talent Go?

While the military includes every type of job description imaginable, veterans without a college education tend to end up in a few specific fields, regardless of their military training. Although many job search websites collect information about job seekers, including whether they've performed military service, that information is not always appropriately conveyed to the employers who use the search websites to look for applicants. There are databases available for veteran-friendly employers to post jobs that give preference to veterans[29] but, often, both employers and veterans are left to find and navigate the websites with minimal assistance. Unfortunately, these databases have recently come into question and been associated with scandal. On top of that, many veterans are not aware of where or how to highlight their military experience on their resumés.

Without the knowledge on how to update a military resumé to a civilian one, and properly highlighting the skills and training they've had, service members aren't able to properly communicate what they know and what they can do to the employers who are open and interested in hiring them. Employers may be looking for specific keywords or certifications, and the veteran may have an equivalent certification or be unaware of those keywords, so the two never connect, although they could be a good match.

People who are transitioning to civilian work from military enlistment may find themselves serving people in the retail or restaurant industries, as truck drivers or local couriers, or in automotive services, construction, or security positions.[30] Depending on the service member's training, a career in technology, engineering, or government positions may be open to them[31] and, regardless of training, the three industries that veterans are most seeking employment in are information technology/information services, defense technologies (including engineering), and government positions.[32] While some veterans transition into police work, healthcare, or firefighting careers that utilize their military training and provide reasonable salaries and benefits, many others find themselves punching a time clock and relying on two or three part-time jobs to make ends meet.

However, while searching for jobs, two out of three (67%) of veterans report that they didn't find work comparable to their military training.[33] The way that job ads are structured, the salesy and buzzword-heavy copy makes it difficult for many veterans to see how the job may be a fit for their skills. Generally, veterans report only applying to job ads where they recognize how their training applies, which means that many veterans likely miss opportunities that are written using unfamiliar words to describe common skills.

Veterans seeking jobs also reported that more than half of the time, they didn't feel that interviewers like recruiters and HR professionals understood their military skills. It was difficult to explain to them how efficiency in their training contributed to the larger mission of the group, or to describe their day-to-day duties in a way that translates to the corporate world. While the current unemployment rate may not be "too bad" for veterans, the fact remains that one in three (33%) feel underemployed.[34] They feel, on some deep level, that they're "worth" more than the job they end up with.

And I agree. When I look around me in my community, in my state of Florida, and across the country, do you know what I don't see veterans becoming? Teachers, professors, artists and performers, marketing directors, and video game developers; I want to see veterans as the law makers, the lesson-givers, and the leaders in our communities. I see them starting businesses, but I want to see them taking those businesses further. I want to see more veteran-owned businesses and fewer veteran employees who feel undervalued. I want to see our veterans achieve the American Dream and their own personal sense of success.

Chapter 3—Campuses Need Students to Lead Each Other

Large Universities Need Leadership

Most large universities recognize that they are a collective of loosely organized, vaguely purposeful, young adults. The amount of work it takes for a university administration to house, schedule, and account for as many as 50,000 individuals requires a massive amount of work and dedication. There is no denying the hard work it takes to maintain the excellence of our American universities, which also rank among some of the top institutions in the world in many regards. And, the truth is, the university administrations know that they need all the help they can get; they know they need strong leaders on campus.

Join a university today and you'll see a number of extracurricular options—join an intramural sport, be a resident assistant or freshman tour guide, join a fraternity or an art or computer programming group.[35] Universities make it a point to offer students many ways to "get involved," and even multiple opportunities to establish themselves as leaders in a community on campus. Many universities are now beginning to explore options of "shared leadership," where there are multiple people sharing the responsibilities of a single role, which is often more conducive to students' busy schedules and the priority on education.[36]

One of the traditional and long-standing paths toward being seen as a "leader" on campus—recognized by other students on campus and beyond—is holding an office in student government. Not only do the members of the student government become involved with and known to their peers on campus, they become known by alumni, outside supporters, and the highest levels of university administration.

The class president or student body president often has direct access to the highest levels of faculty and administration; they often speak at multiple events, including the opening of new facilities, ceremonies for faculty, and graduation. Of all the roles that benefit a young adult far into his or her career, being a university's student body president is at the top of the list in many state universities and private schools across the country.

While somewhat glamorous and certainly a unique on-campus experience, the student body president is often subject to being the poster child for the university's popularity contest. Not only are they required to be upstanding models for their student body, they are also paraded in front of politicians and athletes, both vying for attention and having their attention pulled in every direction. Where this position was once designed as a representative who would help co-ordinate students' needs with the administration's priorities, the position is becoming less about leadership and more about public relations.

The top role of many university student body presidents is now considered to be the "top fundraiser" for the school.[37] According to one report, student body presidents are first and foremost strategists and storytellers, and then they are fundraisers. To prepare for the office, you should have a strong background in finance and money management.

You have to be able to collaborate, and you have to have financial and operational acumen. Last on their long list of the top skills that make a successful university student body president today is that he or she needs to be an "academic and intellectual leader."

What happened to our university student government representation? Is this what we're teaching the future generations of our country—that the people who have titles are better equipped for the position with financial insight than with true leadership skills? It's no wonder that many college students graduate without a sense of how to spot true leaders among their peers. Too many college students today see a storyteller and follow, without realizing that they're being led only toward an illusion of success rather than the reality of it. There is such a lack of team building and true peer-to-peer leadership in many universities' student governments that the overall student body looks elsewhere—to social media, to Hollywood, to trendy entrepreneurs—to find examples of "leadership." What they don't realize is that true leaders are all around them, unable to break into the structures of student government and bring forward a true model of responsible networking and problem-solving.

In studies, leaders on college campuses have been shown to help their peers learn the skills needed to be effective team players.[38] When students feel that their campus is welcoming to all groups of people in positions of leadership, they rate their school as more engaging, and they tend to be more engaged in the resources available to them. Recognition is one of the best ways to motivate today's college students and keep them engaged. With the technology available today, there are more ways than ever for students to become involved in roles of leadership, not only in the school, but in the community. With more engagement of students in the local community, the more popular and successful the school becomes over time.

STUDENT VETERANS IN STUDENT GOVERNMENT

How many of our student veterans are involved in student body politics? How many veterans are represented in the highest levels of their own school administration? According to one study, it may be as little as an average of 11% of student body government association positions are occupied by veterans.[39] At some universities, there may only be a single member of the student body government who has military experience.

While this is a helpful start, and some universities are open to discussing veterans' issues with the veteran organizations on campus, the discussions aren't getting very far. While the universities need strong leaders to help keep their busy student population studying, engaging, and enjoying their college experience, they don't seem to recognize the amazing pool of leaders they already have on campus—the more than 1 million student veterans with unparalleled leadership potential that is left untapped.

Veterans are unique leaders. The experiences of being military personnel make them unique. Veterans have seen and experienced things that traditional students haven't. They may have experienced near-death experiences, and seen friends and colleagues meet tragic, fatal ends on behalf of their service to the country. They have traveled to other countries and have valuable contributions to make to the classroom in discussions of international relations, travel, and human rights.[40]

Not only are they more likely than their civilian peers to engage in the classwork, they are less likely to engage in campus activities and non-study-related get-togethers. They might be more likely to discuss topics with their professors outside of class time, but less likely to join instructors at events or activities that do not take place in the classroom.

THE VALUE OF LEADERSHIP

Recall back to the description of what it takes to be a great student body president nowadays. Are we really okay with the fact that being an "academic and intellectual leader" is the lowest set of skills on that list? The student body president is someone who represents the study body to the monetary interests of the school, so they have to be able to speak the language of money, but do they have to speak the language of the study body? Do they have to actually lead the student body in any of the maneuvers they perform?

I found that those questions were hard to answer, as each school does things its own way.[41] One thing that became clear to me, though, is the lack of direct structured connection between any levels of student body government and the actual students that they "governed." Unlike military leadership, there is no chain between the people who represent them to the money managers and financiers for the school and the students who are staying up late, grinding their gears, and struggling to get by.

Veterans on college campuses are forgotten leaders. In the military, leadership has value. From the highest generals through all levels of enlistment, leadership is a value that is woven through every fiber of our military. The military is a meritocracy—rewarding true leaders with promotions and regalia based on their merit, based on their real-world actions. On college campuses, it is a wildly different environment.

Even at the most veteran-friendly universities, where they may have hundreds or thousands of veterans enrolled, only a dozen show up for their events. By getting them engaged in the gaps around campus, including valuable positions of leadership in sports, organizations, and student government, universities could greatly benefit.

Chapter 4—Vets Become Isolated

As we've discussed, one of the biggest concerns for our veterans on college campuses is their feeling of isolation.[42] This feeling, combined with being overloaded with schoolwork, contributes to depression, anxiety, and loneliness.

While surrounded by thousands of other people, veterans may feel like they've been left on an island by themselves. They can't truly connect with others because of their age and lifestyle differences. But it's not just the age difference that pushes them apart from other students; they have also experienced vastly different life choices and events, which can be sensitive subjects that are difficult to tactfully discuss with others.

In addition to the disconnect with their classmates, student veterans often feel ignored or disconnected from their instructors and professors. Veterans come into contact with all levels of faculty, from teachers' assistants who may be about their same age, to tenured professors who are decades older with a very different view of military life than theirs, based on outdated or historical perspectives. Many of the more academic professors want to discuss the intellectual aspects of military life, which may or may not be a welcome topic to many veterans, making them feel further isolated from the faculty.

VETERANS DISCONNECTED FROM OTHER STUDENTS

Dealing with Civilian Peers

In addition to the age difference, which overall can make student veterans view their classmates as immature, they become disconnected from their peers in other ways as well. As we've discussed, veterans often have family and employment obligations and don't live on campus, which makes them outsiders from the traditional student experience. While others can bond over living conditions in the dorms or events the veteran wasn't able to attend, veterans can't relate to them on these day-to-day, simple experiences.

Often, when someone's attention is called to a veteran's military service, other people will immediately try to connect on that level. Many college students may not have had the chance to speak with a military service member before and, in an awkward, immature attempt to connect, they may ask the veteran some highly personal questions that can make the veteran uncomfortable or trigger a PTSD emotional reaction.

In recent studies, researchers found that many veterans experience "intrusive or unpleasant" interactions with non-veteran peers, including having the other person ask the veteran if he or she had ever killed anyone or seen someone die while in a combat situation. Many veterans who have seen combat have experienced death first-hand, and don't like to relive or remember those experiences in a safe, yet unfamiliar setting, such as a college classroom. This can be even more difficult if the veteran is asked about his or her experience in front of a group, which happens not only from insensitive or uneducated peers, but can also come from uncomfortable questions asked by an instructor.

Young adults, especially young men, may have a tendency to glorify and romanticize war, thinking it is "cool" to kill someone, or "dramatic" to see someone die. Non-veterans may have an image of death that is rooted in military-style video games or Hollywood depictions. The true veteran knows that battle is neither "cool" nor "dramatic" in an entertaining way. Unfortunately, some of their peers place them in a position to have to defend this knowledge, hard-gained from personal experience.

It can take some helpful therapeutic techniques to make sure that all student veterans are able to calm and control any anxiety and respond to their peers. If this is something that many of our veterans are encountering on college campuses, they should have psychological and emotional support services on those same campuses to help them in a moment of crisis when they have been triggered by someone on campus, causing them to relive a painful or terrifying experience.

Connecting with Other Student Veterans

In addition to the disconnect with non-veteran students, veterans also feel disconnected from each other on college campuses. Some veterans report that they can identify the other vets on campus because of the mannerisms, dress, and lingo they use, but they don't strike out and introduce themselves. It is difficult enough to introduce yourself to someone else at a college campus, and some veterans are self-conscious about whether to approach someone else on the basis of military service alone.

How do you know what to say to the other person? Often, veterans can walk up to one another and say, "What branch were you in?" as an easy ice-breaker, but there can still be tension surrounding the introduction. The two veterans could have served in vastly different branches or years apart; they could have vast differences in rank, which causes its own unique dynamic. It might be uncomfortable for them to speak about their experiences or in a more casual military terminology with non-veteran students around. While military experiences are a good jumping-off point for conversation when two veterans meet, colleges don't make it easy for veterans to find one another.

When they first register, many veterans aren't informed about any veteran organizations on campus unless they think to ask, or the information is given to them among a thick packet of other paperwork, or it's buried somewhere in the orientation publications. In an ideal world, every veteran would read through this information in full detail, but let's be real. We know that these students already are obligated to family and employment and, in an effort to prioritize their registration, they may not notice all the details of their orientation books.

If more campuses had more successful and easily accessible veteran centers, and if veterans were made more immediately aware of this as a safe, open space to connect with other veterans, veterans could begin the essential connections to fight the isolation so prevalent in their experience.

STUDENT VETERANS DISCONNECTED FROM FACULTY

A university's "faculty" can be made up of many part-time and full-time instructors who are involved in the university to widely varying extents. Unlike military life, where everyone is fully invested, university employment includes a range of instructors who are employees, subject to come and go at will, ranging from some graduate students who teach one or two classes to receive a stipend for their tuition, to salaried, tenured professors who are recognized as academic leaders in their fields of study. In between, there are associate professors, assistant professors, and adjunct professors, not to mention research assistants and laboratory technicians. It can be very confusing for a veteran to figure out which person is going to be the most helpful to answer questions.

On the other hand, instructors may not be able to identify the veterans and, even if they can tell who the veterans are, they may not understand the different needs of that slice of the student population. In my research, I found some stories of instructors who asked the veterans in their class to stand up so the other students could applaud them for their service. One veteran reported that it was "nice" although unexpected, and it was certainly a singular experience during his entire college career.

According to the report, student veterans don't necessarily want to be recognized for their service—they don't necessarily want to be called out or have attention drawn to them for it in front of their civilian co-students—but they do want the teachers to recognize that they are non-traditional students. Because of the varied levels within the hierarchy, dedication, and involvement of their instructors, the veterans report that the instructors tend to see all their students "the same," and the veterans have to particularly point out that their situations are unique. Sometimes, even then, veterans have difficulty getting the recognition from their instructors regarding their work ethic, unique needs and experiences, and other circumstances that make them different from the younger, traditional students.[43]

DISCUSSING POLITICS WITH OTHERS ON CAMPUS

Universities may have earned a reputation for being "liberal" but, in my research, I found that it's more complicated than that. There is a wide range of ideologies on a single college campus, and a wide range of very different college campuses for veterans to choose from, so it's not fair to assume that all veterans deal with clashes between "liberal" and "conservative" politics on college campuses.

While some campuses may promote themselves as conservative or veteran-friendly, there are other campuses that pride themselves on having an anti-military sentiment and, at both types of campus, there are many different mindsets. No matter where our veterans choose to attend school, they are very likely to encounter political discussions that make them uncomfortable.

Because of this, many veterans report feeling shy about discussing their military service at a college campus. They feel like neither their classmates nor their instructors can relate to their experiences, which often affect their personal politics.[44]

The politics of service members and non-veterans can vary widely. When military actions are discussed on campus, those who served may find that their opinion is not popular, or even unwelcome, and that it doesn't matter if their opinion is better informed than others or not. Many people don't understand that "the military" is not a single, collective unit, but several co-operative branches. Some people make sweeping generalizations about what the military "should" do, without any consideration for the real actions of real people that lead to those large-scale results. Veterans have a more thorough understanding of this, which can cause a disconnect between them and the other students. This can be especially true for veterans who have served post-9/11 because of the deep and often dividing politics regarding U.S. actions since that fateful day.

Remember how I earlier mentioned that no U.S. president has served in the military since the 1970s? Throughout all levels of society, veterans may feel that there is a disconnect between leadership and military reality. On college campuses, many of their peers are highly influenced by the drama of national politics that, for many veterans is less "entertainment" and more real-life, boots-on-the-ground fear for their friends who are still on active duty. While service members may see themselves and their companions as warriors and respect them for the sacrifices they continue to make, many of their fellow college students do not, and our hard-working, service-oriented veterans bear harassment or tension based around their life choices.

Chapter 5—Problems with Current Resources

Are There Current Student Veterans Groups?

The short answer to this question is: yes, in name. There are many groups that promote themselves as serving the student veteran population, but my research has shown me that schools have no real organization to support this student population.

When we look at the current student veteran organizations, they have their presence on colleges, but nothing they are doing is working. They are not actively engaging their student veterans, are not offering the kind of support the veterans truly need, and what support they *can* offer is insufficient. In their defense, how could they truly be efficient? One of the major student veteran organizations has a central office in Washington, D.C. made up of a staff of only 25. Twenty-five people are clearly insufficient to help co-ordinate services for the 1 million and more veterans on our college campuses.[45]

While I would love to say that I've found that many college administrators are genuinely invested in supporting student veterans through their college careers, the truth is that I have found that college administrators are the gatekeepers who are more interested in their jobs than in building real programs that support our veterans.

Schools love to give the illusion that everything is great, but there is a lack of participation, very little money, and few staff, without vision or support. Colleges love G.I. Bill money, and they all say that they are the friendliest environment for veterans but, in interviewing veterans from multiple campuses, I have found that the reality often falls far short of the image they portray.

It's not only the school administrators' fault, as individual chapters of large national organizations receive little to no help—financial or otherwise. For example, the largest student veteran organization boasts just two scholarships on their website—for $10,000 each. They are proud to promote that they have a network of more than 15,000 chapters. If spread evenly, that scholarship money would be less than $1,000 per chapter, but that might be a boost to their current budgets, according to some of the reports we received from chapter members and organizers.[46]

So how far does this type of organizational "help" really go? With more than 1 million student veterans enrolled in schools across America, with this organization claiming that 700,000 of those veterans are members, who are they really helping?

WHAT SERVICES SHOULD LOOK LIKE

The American Council on Education states that the presence of a strong student veteran organization on campus is the "best practice" that all campuses should strive for.[47] A supportive, engaging organization could be linked to academic success, as well as the much-needed peer-to-peer support and socialization that many veterans crave.

One major factor is whether there is a vet center on campus. At colleges that have a designated space for student veterans, the vet center can become the place for them to study and socialize. While some student veteran organizations are working to build vet centers at more colleges, there are many campuses that have only a single designated desk in a busy student center, or a single room in a maze-like building, that is set aside as a specific space for student veterans to meet, lounge, and mingle.

This type of student veteran center might be separate from the office where student veterans can receive direct support services from knowledgeable school administrators. While veterans certainly appreciate a place where they can quietly study or relax and relieve their anxiety about being around non-veteran students, veterans also need an office where they can get assistance filling out paperwork, registering for classes, get advice on financial aid and medical processes and resources, as well as other valuable guidance.

Many college campuses do not offer such a resource center or, if they do have an office where veterans can go, expecting guidance, the veterans who visit often find it staffed by part-time interns and other students—people who can't truly provide more than the most basic answers to their questions. Unfortunately, different veteran groups often struggle for attention on college campuses, competing among themselves.[48] This can leave the current student veteran resource centers in a position where they find their chapter presidents on campus, and then they have little to no budget to execute any truly impactful ideas.

I'm sorry to report that the campuses I visited during my research all had student veteran resource centers, with a paid director and a staff of part-time student veterans, but without any budget and with a total lack of vision.

When executed properly, a successful student veteran organization should help veterans feel more engaged in student life. Right now, the organizations that exist to help student veterans are seeing very low participation numbers—generally less than 10% of the veterans enrolled on their particular campus. The participation is virtually non-existent because the services they offer aren't relevant to the veterans themselves and don't resonate within the student veterans' community. For example, if one of the services the veterans' office offers is to provide discounted tickets to movie theaters, restaurants, or local entertainment and attractions, how valuable is that service compared to the type of support they could be offering? Seems to me the veterans could get the same type of service from Groupon or one of the other dozens of online discount-shopping websites, and the veterans' center should focus on offering more substantial support.

Student veterans need a great support network; they need friends they can relate to.

When student veterans connect, they can support each other with academic and personal struggles, often approaching problems using the same methodology and techniques they learned in military training. Having a place on campus where they can connect with others keeps them engaged and more likely to succeed in college. Having the proper support services proves even more valuable—it can help prevent student veterans from dropping out, save them valuable time and money by pointing them in the right direction early in their search and, ultimately, change their lives.[49]

The services on campuses to help prevent veterans from falling behind their peers should be more comprehensive, offering tutoring, mentoring, and connections with local businesses. After coming from a military culture that teaches service members to "adapt and overcome" when challenged, it can be difficult to see the benefit of reaching out for help in the process of adapting.[50] And, if they decide they want to reach out, it can be difficult for them to know where to go on campus or to make the time in their schedules to get there. However, if these valuable services were offered at the veterans' center, colleges would likely see a large increase in how many veterans utilize the center, which could snowball into greater results for the veterans individually and the group collectively.

Chapter 6—Stories from Veterans

While preparing my materials for this book, I wanted to interview as many veterans as I could about their experiences. Research was helpful to understand the broad spectrum of issues, but what about the individuals? Trends are made up of people, and any information that shows how an issue impacts a group also should show some measure of a person's individual experience, but it can't capture everything.

Many people were afraid to speak out "on the record." They told me their stories, but they were not interested in "drawing any fire" or putting themselves "in hot water" by making statements that could be seen in a poor light, either by the VA or by their college. Many people shared their support for the message and agreed with the needs that SVF is working to meet; however, they were concerned about some type of retribution should their name become associated with criticism of the large systems of which they are members.

Three of the veterans I spoke with who were gracious enough to put their names on record offered extremely valuable insight into the realities that student veterans face. The men have stories that are very different in some ways, and very much the same in other ways. All these men's stories highlight many of the issues discussed to this point—but let's put some names on those data points, shall we?

Interview with Michael Cullen

Personal History

"Full disclosure: I am on the board of the Student Veterans Foundation." Michael Cullen has been working hard to provide support for veterans for years, because he knows just how difficult it can be for a veteran who is just transitioning out of the military.

After his six-year enlistment with the Marine Corps ended in 1996, Mike felt "like a lost, soaking wet cat." He found that he got lost in the familiar territory of the civilian world he used to know, remembering how, "A lot of the short-cuts I had memorized had disappeared." When he enlisted, Mike intended to attend college during his active duty time, but had only managed to complete one class before his enlistment ended. He immediately sought out the educational benefits through the VA and was disappointed to find out that the support "wasn't very deep." That is, until he discovered and was enrolled in the VA's vocational rehabilitation program, which offered greater support and assistance to the former Marine.

Mike's enlistment ended when he was in Quantico, Virginia and, like many military service members, Mike returned to his home in central Florida. "If you are enlisted when you first get out, you don't have a lot of money, so you go where it's safe and comfortable. If you're an officer, it's different but, for me, there was no way I could afford not to go home." After a brief stint at his family's house, where a family friend had helped set him up with a blue-collar job, he didn't want to get dragged down and stuck in a rut. He still had plans to succeed so he enrolled at Santa Fe Community College in Gainesville, Florida, and started chasing his dreams.

Once accepted into the vocational rehabilitation program, Mike was assigned a counselor at the VA who was very supportive of his situation and his needs. "We didn't talk all the time," he said. "We would check in once every three to six months, and I could reach out when I had a need. The challenge that I faced was finding support on campus." Looking for the *esprit de corps* and camaraderie he experienced during his enlistment, Mike developed a relationship with a young lady who was also a veteran and, through her, he became connected with the broader veteran community at the college.

"Vocational rehab was a great program, but I only happened to find it by accident. Something like SVF would have helped open doors and would have pointed me in the right direction."

Mike recalls the difficulty of making the transition on his own. Moving from a structured environment like the one in the Marine Corps to one where you have to create your own structure was incredibly difficult and even overwhelming at times.

"The Marine Corps is a lot of 'hurry up and wait'—but you know where you need to be, when to be there, and how to present yourself when you get there. When you go to college, it's a process of self-discovery that begins with identifying the school itself. Which school will you attend? What program? Then there's registration, orientation, acceptance, scheduling classes—then what happens? As a student, you're on your own but, when you add in the layers of complexity, it compounds any anxiety a veteran feels in the first few days of full-time college attendance. You have to figure out where to live, and how to get around. They're positive stressors, but they're still stressors."

At Santa Fe Community College, Mike felt supported. They had a veterans' office, which he remembers visiting immediately, and he was pleasantly surprised to find they had veterans, not civilians, working in the office. "Having a vet support me was great—albeit, it didn't last very long but, while working with that office, I had a place to go and connect, which made it easier to go to campus, frankly." However, he feels like most campuses don't provide this level of support, instead describing how the majority don't do anything more than "hang a sign."

It took ten long years, full of mishaps and missteps, before Mike completed his bachelor's degree in computer science. During that time, Mike got married and became a father, and he and his family relocated to Orlando, where he enrolled at Rollins College. When he arrived at Rollins, he found that the support was even less than what he had received at the community college, which contributed to the lengthy amount of time he spent working toward his degree.

Once he completed his bachelor's degree, Mike was accepted for the Master's in Business Administration program at Rollins and, working hard to complete that degree much more quickly, he completed the MBA program in 2008.

Mike recalled the multiple struggles he encountered over the decade of working toward his degrees. "I have never been enrolled in college and not worked full-time, including my MBA program," he said. "I had a family I needed to provide for, and I'm not talking about a 40-hour working week. I'm talking about working 60 to 80 hours per week, and then still having the commitment to get my graduate degree. They say the hardest job in the military is for the spouses and family, and I found out that, even out of the military, I needed my family to be supportive. They had to have the ability to see the light at the end of the tunnel."

Today, Mike and his family live outside of Orlando. He is a partner in a promotional and branding products company, as well as being a management consultant for C-level executives. A busy, successful entrepreneur, Mike is proof that education is what leads to true opportunity.

Lessons & Impacts

Based on his experience, Mike believes there's an immediate need to impact veterans, but that their success will ultimately depend on an overarching strategy. "How do we change how vets go to college and how do we change the cost of college for the broader community?"

Commenting on how the cost of college has become "brutal" for everything, he noted the differences between the costs in 1996 and in 2008, which had more than doubled. "The rate of growth [for the cost of college] has far exceeded the savings rate, the interest rate, inflation – all of it. We need legislation." He is passionate and ready to act, with big goals for how SVF will make an impact.

Specifically, Mike believes that officers leave the military in a different financial position than enlisted service members. He wants to close that gap and make it easier for enlisted personnel to succeed. He knows from personal experience that many young student veterans return home to live with family and, while they may not intend to be a financial or emotional burden on their loved ones, their lack of direction and difficulties with transitioning into civilian life can create tension.

"Some veterans might find a roommate, but my friends and I all went home where it was comfortable. We relied on our families to reintegrate into civilian life, and we didn't have a huge community to engage. My close relationships in the Marine Corps were severed, except for occasional reunions. Some veterans choose campuses far away from their hometowns, and they start craving relationships and ways to connect, and I don't mean having an office with free coffee and an intern. If they have someone sitting in the office who said, 'Do you want to talk?' I hated that. I wasn't a victim. I wasn't a hero. I was just someone who was now a citizen after leaving the Marine Corps, trying to better myself."

As a member of the SVF board, Mike is passionate about ensuring that the majority of money in the SVF budget, except for operating costs, should be given back to the vets themselves. From his research, he knows that most veterans' organizations on college campuses don't have large budgets, and he is creating a budget for SVF that will put money into offsetting and defraying the costs of college for future student veterans.

"The SVF could pursue multiple threads to improve life for vets overall. We could lobby to change the rate of growth for college tuition. We could look into making an impact on how college tuition is moving and the associated fees and costs. SVF can also offer scholarships to veterans to ease their financial burden. It comes down to fundraising, grants, and the ability to distribute the funds that are provided."

The VA still offers the vocational rehab program, and Mike would still recommend it for any veteran who qualifies, but he also wants to see the on-campus resources at SVF connected with the programs at the VA. He wants the vets going through the VA to know that, when they arrive at campus, there will be more help for them.

Advice & Looking Forward

"There isn't one solution—it's really about developing a relationship." Mike sees the resources that are available to veterans in the community, but he knows that many vets don't know where to reach out, don't even know those resources are available. And he sees a variety of ways that SVF can have an immediate impact for the student veterans who are on campus now, while still fighting for benefits for all student veterans in the future.

"I believe every campus should be pushed to accept Tricare. I had to drive to Tampa a few times to get appointments, and I don't see any reason why we shouldn't be treating our veterans on campus. Basic, simple medical care should be available. Many prescriptions can be filled and mailed out through the VA, unless it's a high-control substance. For most routine prescriptions, there are resources available. If I'm a student veteran and I'm engaged and know about the resources, then my life just got easier. It's as simple as connecting the dots. Most veterans just don't know how to draw out the line from one to the next, and it's not always a straight line."

One resource that Mike would like to see implemented immediately is veteran book drops. He feels that, "All too often, students graduate and hold onto their books for nostalgia or resources. What do you need them for? You have Google. In some cases, there's money to be made from the sale of donated goods, and those funds could be retained for vets."

In addition, he knows how central fundraising will be to the success of SVF but, as a corporate marketing and branding expert, he also knows how easy promotion and awareness can be when done right. "There's so many ways to raise funds," he said, listing off several ideas—T-shirts, branded USB drives, coffee mugs. All the things college students use and need. "When you're on campus and see something like a branded T-shirt in the window of an office with a sign, that adds weight and credibility."

Mike works from the belief that the success of a program like the Student Veterans Foundation will be built on creating a community, not just on a single campus, but a community that's connected across all college campuses. Large university branches of SVF should connect with the branches at smaller colleges through social media and coordinated live events. "All of them have a student vet population," he said. "Are they talking? Are they broadening their services and their network? Are they connecting?"

Overall, no matter what type of veteran, no matter what branch they were enlisted in, and no matter what their long-term dream, Mike is rooted in the idea that every veteran can be successful. "Whether they're working toward a certification in IT or to be a truck driver or mechanic, or if they're going to college for a traditional bachelor's degree or two-year degree. If we help them connect the dots between where they are and where they want to be, they will build the lives they want to live."

INTERVIEW WITH SHERIFF PAYTON GRINNELL

Personal History

In 1991, Payton Grinnell was transitioning out of the Marine Corps into civilian life. He calls the experience "chaotic." Throughout his military service, including deployment during the Persian Gulf conflict, he had dreamed of going into a career with the secret service, one day hoping to work his way to being a special agent. During the conflict, there had been an involuntary extension of service, which interrupted his application for the secret service. Although Grinnell had timed things correctly so the fifteen-month-long application process would line up with his enlistment end date, the involuntary extension made him ineligible and put a halt on the application process.

"They told me that, when I got out, I could reapply. It takes so long, because it's very rigorous screening—and rightly so—but because of the involuntary extension I had to decline my job offer from the secret service."

Because his wife was attending George Washington University in Washington, D.C. on a swimming scholarship, the young vet from Lake County, Florida, moved there to be with her, without knowing anyone else in town or having any other kind of local support system. After the Persian Gulf conflict ended, there was a mass exodus of military service members in May of 1991. As Grinnell describes it, the job market was highly competitive in D.C., and he was at a disadvantage. He found that many of the veterans he was competing against for jobs had already completed their college degrees, either before they enlisted or during their enlistment. "I was simply unemployable," he said. For months, Grinnell couldn't get hired.

Grinnell got odd jobs, popping popcorn at a movie theater and waiting tables, then tending bar for a few months, before he decided that going back to school was the right long-term decision. Knowing that he wanted to work in law enforcement, Grinnell enrolled at Northern Virginia Community College, seeking an Applied Associates Degree in criminal justice.

"If I could go back and do it differently, I would, but I didn't have anyone to talk to about this. I thought at the time that, if you want to work in the criminal justice system, you need a degree in criminal justice, but I found out that's just not the case. A business degree, political science degree, management degree—all those are applicable. You can use all those skills. And, in the event that you get hurt in the line of duty and can't be a law enforcement officer anymore, then you have something to fall back on."

Getting to the college campus and navigating what was required of him was difficult. While working two jobs and supporting his wife, Grinnell recalls that he didn't know anyone or have a service he could turn to.

"I was trying to get help, structure, and guidance. I had to find my own way. I wasted a lot of time trying to get from point A to point B whereas, if there had been an organization I could turn to, it would have made that transition easier."

He didn't know who to turn to for administrative help, so if he had veterans benefits available to attend school, he never applied for them. He recalls being older than the "typical" student, still sporting his high-and-tight haircut, and feels like he was always looked at as "different." Luckily for Payton Grinnell, a seasoned veteran of the D.C. Metro Police took him "under his wing." It was one of Grinnell's adjunct professors, and he went out of his way to help Grinnell feel at home.

"He was a homicide investigator, probably a year or two from retirement, and he was very helpful as far as making sure that I felt a part of the college culture and the campus life. He introduced me to some of the faculty and staff there, and he let them know that I was a guy who had just got back from deployment and was trying to land a law enforcement job. 'We need to help him out,' he basically told them on my behalf."

When his wife graduated from the university, the couple decided to return to their roots in central Florida. Grinnell put in to transfer, and the two moved back to Lake County. He decided to complete his bachelor's degree in Organizational Management, then faced an administrative hiccup that required him to repeat some classes he had taken in Virginia. Through a partnership between Lake Technical College and Warner University, the sheriff completed his bachelor's degree and began his employment with the Lake County Sheriff's Office in 1994.

In 2018, Sheriff Grinnell once again enrolled as a university student, this time, to pursue his Master's degree in Criminal Justice. He is one of a handful of students enrolled in the Orlando-based satellite campus of Columbia College, which houses its main campus in Missouri. He is finding his master's program easier to tackle, because the size of the campus and its community is much more manageable and familiar.

"I'm in class with executives and experienced law enforcement professionals who are in my age group. We're all settled in life and family, the kids are out of high school, and now we're finding it convenient to go to college a few nights a week and work toward our higher education. I'm in there with my peers, and it's very comfortable. Some students are younger, but the majority of my classmates have circumstances similar to mine. We're supportive. We do study groups, meet up and prepare for exams, and help each other with papers."

It's a different educational experience, because of age, technology, and so many other factors but, despite all that, the sheriff tells me that, if there was somewhere to go on campus to meet up with other veterans, he would definitely go there.

Lessons & Impacts

Looking back on what made his transition from military to civilian life, and especially student life, so difficult, the sheriff recalls how difficult the lack of structure was for him.

"You come from a structured lifestyle where your day is laid out for you, from the time you rise to the time you go to bed, and now, all of a sudden, you don't have that. You may be trying to get a job and, even if you're not really spinning your wheels, it feels that way, because you just don't see closure and accomplishment right away. I remember that being difficult."

The sheriff credits his wife for helping him through the transition, but he knows first-hand that there are many young men and women exiting the military, seeking direction, who don't have a spouse or local loved ones to rely on. Now, he works to be that same mentor, taking young veterans under his wing, the way his adjunct professor did for him all those years ago.

The Lake County Sheriff's Office partners with the Lake Sumter Technical College for a direct pipeline into law enforcement careers. He works as a mentor and teacher to students—many of whom are veterans—hoping to lead by example and show them a clear message of structure and success. He oversees the coordination services at the law enforcement academy at the technical college, making sure that any veterans in the program have their training paid for through their G.I. Bill. They offer extensive administrative support.

"It works out well, because the academy's training and certification process is structured. The on-campus structure of the academy is regimented, which makes the transition easier for them. But not so with a general degree at a state college or public university. I think it's when you get outside of the public safety profession—when you get into general education—it's more difficult for veterans to navigate. There's a lot of freedom. They're responsible for their own calendar. It's a lot harder."

The key factor that Sheriff Grinnell finds contributes to the success of veterans who enter his team? A feeling of inclusion. A sense that they're being included in what's going on. He recognizes how the age gap between many veterans and their fellow students at a traditional campus could contribute to a feeling of exclusion. "Especially if they're older," he says, "maybe they won't be involved in a fraternity or sorority on campus. But maybe they would be more likely to join a program of veterans, where they could talk with people with something to relate to and be with like-minded individuals. I know I would." That's why it's important to the sheriff that he provide that space for veterans to introduce themselves to one another and to feel at home at his local police academy.

Advice & Looking Forward

If there was one message I took away from my discussion with Sheriff Grinnell, it's that little actions can have a huge impact. He thinks that, if universities and colleges across the country offered a veteran orientation seminar, it would be incredibly helpful. Not only would it give veterans on campus a chance to connect with their local brother (and sister) hood, it would provide them with valuable information that other students may already have at their disposal.

In the gap between completing his studies in 1994 and re-entering higher education in 2018, there were huge technological advances in the classroom. The sheriff knows first-hand how some veterans have missed the lesson on how to use the newest technology because they were deployed or it was something they simply weren't aware of. He feels like an orientation when he re-enrolled would have been invaluable.

"Today, with some of these applications, things are much more streamlined. But those are things that require instruction, and student veterans first need to know they're available before they can use them. I wouldn't have thought to look for this software or have been able to benefit from all the technology available if it hadn't been brought to my attention by someone in class. Technology has come a long way—and it's just one of the things that veterans need to know is out there for them."

As a veteran, he points out, "you just don't know what things are" on a college campus.

"I had to learn what a student center was and what the different buildings on campus were. If there had been a veterans' building or lounge or office, I would have gone there first to get a sense of comfort and hopefully be able to connect with a mentor or someone who could show me the ropes. I would go for the camaraderie, so we could exchange phone numbers and go through the educational process together. We may have never met before, but the fact they are veterans is what matters. Veterans need to connect. It gives them a sense that 'I'm out in the real world, but I'm alongside my brothers and sisters.' Then, they don't feel alone."

Even now, in his fifties and after decades of experience and accolades, Sheriff Payton Grinnell is still looking for ways to connect with other veterans and learn from them.

Interview with Mark Singleton

Personal Story

After a fourteen-year enlistment in the Air Force that began in 1980, Mark Singleton transitioned back into civilian life in 1994. He had grown up as a dependent and well-acquainted with military life—as his father, uncles, step-father, and many other family members were service members throughout his childhood.

When he was a teenager, his parents were stationed in South Carolina. Mark was attending a private military school in Virginia when his father got orders to be stationed in the Philippines. "It didn't bother me," he said. "I figured I would stay in school and just go visit them over the summers." But his parents didn't support that plan and, in a teenage rage, Mark dropped out of school entirely. After the family moved to the Philippines, Mark's parents were able to talk him into re-enrolling in school there. However, that didn't work out, either, and he dropped out of school again.

"Then I did the logical thing that any seventeen-year-old with no diploma would do—I enlisted in the Air Force. I thoroughly enjoyed it for the first fourteen years. I was in military intelligence. It was great."

When presented with the opportunity to retire after a fifteen-year enlistment, Mark applied for the Senate-sponsored initiative. However, the Pentagon rejected his application for retirement, stating that his career field was too critical. But, when a second initiative offered a retirement bonus, he pushed quickly to be approved for that program. Looking back, he realizes that when he made that hasty decision in October of 1994, he was ill-prepared for the transition.

Mark recalls working at small manual labor jobs, bouncing around from one industry to another for years. He never really found a career he could enjoy, one that could provide a sufficient life for his wife and three children. Having been trained in specialized skills pertaining to military intelligence, he felt like his skill set didn't apply to any of the jobs in his area. "Unless I wanted to move to a place like D.C., which I didn't want to do, I couldn't find anything in my field." In addition to professional skills, Mark recalls that he didn't have a personal skill set that adapted well to the civilian world, either.

"My life had always been structured for me. I didn't have to plan much and, when I had total freedom without those boundaries, I didn't handle that transition well. I wasn't aware of any transition placement services to help. After I got out, there was very little in terms of resource from the VA or anybody. No legal assistance or financial literacy assistance. It changed my whole family."

Over the years, the family relocated to Las Vegas, then Texas, and Mark started to shift his career path toward sales. With his propensity to excel, his jobs began to show increasing economic gain—they started paying better—but he was not well disciplined with the income, and he and his wife ran into financial trouble.

In the mid-2000s, Mark wanted to go back to school, but there didn't seem to be enough money. Because of the year of his enlistment, he fell in a window of time when many service members were not offered extended educational benefits, and his benefits had expired. He found out that the qualifications had been difficult to meet to begin with, but his opportunity window had passed to take advantage of any G.I. Bill benefits. Without proper support services, and having to pay for school on his own dime, the financial troubles ruptured his marriage of thirty-three years, leading to a painful divorce.

Sometime after, in Houston, Mark was working as the director of an art gallery when he met the woman who would become his second wife. One of the things that connected them immediately was their military service; when they met, she was still on active duty with the Army. After they married, they moved to San Antonio where she completed her enlistment before she retired as a fully disabled veteran.

To further their opportunities together, Mark and his wife decided to both re-enroll in school. Currently, he is at Florida State University working on a dual bachelor's degree in sociology and psychology. After completing his undergraduate studies, he plans to apply to the FSU graduate school for a Master's degree in Sports Psychology. His wife is enrolled in a dual bachelor's degree program as well, studying Japanese and Greek, with plans to pursue a second career as a professional translator once her education is complete.

"We're non-traditional students," he laughs. In their fifties, they made their decisions about what college to apply for based on one factor that many traditional students don't take into consideration—bowling. "I wanted to get into collegiate bowling, so one of my criteria was to find a program that had a top-notch coach. The coach [at FSU] has won a national championship."

In addition to looking for a "bowling school," Mark and his wife did look for two criteria that many traditional students also consider—it had also to be a school with a "sound academic reputation, and within a few hours driving distance from the beach."

Mark sees his interest in bowling and beach activities as overlapping with larger issues in sports psychology—his area of study—dealing with athleticism and overall life success. His goal is to become a performance enhancement coach for high school and collegiate athletes, or any athletes in their teens and early twenties, and help them improve their lives in areas that are not sports-related.

"My contention is that the processes by which you become a champion athlete are the same processes as being a superior accountant or mother or high-performing artist or musician—anything you choose to do. It's going to be largely the same processes, which seems to always break down into three questions: *Where are you now? Where do you want to be? And how do we connect the dots?* I want to help student athletes ask themselves these questions and change their mindsets. I'm not beyond helping anybody."

This drive and dedication toward impacting the lives of children with incredible athletic talents discover their other potential is what keeps Mark working hard every day to earn his degrees, despite the challenges he is facing in his situation as a non-traditional student veteran.

Lessons & Impact

The first two years that Mark and his wife lived in Tallahassee, before he transferred from the local community college to FSU, were a roller coaster. He and his wife both battle medical issues resulting from their service. Both have ongoing medical needs that require prescriptions and regular check-ups, and they discovered that Tallahassee would provide more challenges to accommodate those needs than they had been presented with in Texas.

Tallahassee, the capital city of Florida, is a mid-sized town of about 200,000 people. It accommodates both a large student population from FSU and FAMU, as well as a high number of state and national politicians. It's not a large city, but it's not a one-horse town, either. In this medium-sized, modern-day city, Mark has described his experience with getting medical services as a "nightmare." There aren't many doctors who accept his VA medical insurance, and the few who do are an inconvenient distance away.

"Long story short," he says, after describing the search he went through, "I found an office with two doctors about an hour away. They sent an application that had me fill out my entire life's medical history. Once I met the privilege of being eligible for their services, then I get to drive an hour to see them and an hour to return home."

After a tree fell during a hurricane and severed their mobile home while they were both inside, his wife's PTSD began to affect her daily life.

"There were no visible injuries. The first thing I checked was our physical safety, and we were okay. My wife handled it well. At first."

Mark and his wife were living on a stipend for educational assistance they receive because of his wife's disability, but he says it's not a living wage (it's about what someone who earns the minimum wage in Florida makes when working full-time).The community college offered free counseling from unlicensed coordinators, and that was the best counseling services that Mark could find for himself or his wife, based on their financial situation. "It wasn't a psychiatrist or an M.D., but it was enough care to help us manage through the school year," he said.

Mark then tells me how difficult it was to get acceptance into a major state university when he was ready to transfer. They only have so many seats, and their admissions standards are highly competitive, allowing for very little insight beyond the numbers on the page. For an older veteran, whose test scores may be lost or outdated according to the new system, there is a lot of extra explaining to do on the application and admissions forms.

For someone who has traveled internationally in the past ten years, there are additional concerns and hoops to jump through. For someone whose credit is not freshly minted, school loan applications can result in a pile of rejection letters and, for someone who has not sat and written an application essay in decades, the personal statements and letters of intent that are required during the application can be daunting or explosive challenges. The application process at the university level, compared with that of the community college level, was unexpectedly much more complicated.

After four declined applications and a few heated exchanges with the admissions office, Mark was accepted and enrolled as a student at FSU in the fall semester of 2019; however, once he arrived on the FSU campus, Mark was disappointed to discover that the on-campus facilities also did not accept his veteran's medical insurance, nor would they accept the unofficial diagnoses of his and his wife's psychological need for counseling.

"I tried to let the school know that I needed help, but my past counseling wasn't adequate to establish a 'need' and a diagnosis, so they're unwilling to recognize my ailment. They offered me some free counseling similar to what I received at the community college because I told them it was so successful for me there."

While being a member of the veterans' organization on campus is helping, Mark sees the opportunities for growth and the potential to do even more for our veterans on college campuses.

Advice & Looking Forward

I asked Mark specifically what he thinks SVF can do differently—how we can support student veterans in their daily life struggles in a way that will make a huge impact.

"Find the gaps," he told me. "A rising tide raises all boats and, if you can offer services and support that fill the spots that are poorly served now, you will find great opportunity."

For Mark, the most pressing issues for life as a student veteran revolve around access to quality, convenient medical care, as well as supplementary materials that support his education—books, note-books, and memory cards for his computer. The cost of school supplies can take a toll on someone financially limited when every dollar counts and, for dedicated and ambitious students such as Mark, the costs of pursuing the kind of education he strives for are high. The goals are worthy, though, so the costs of supporting him to reach them are minimal by comparison.

Mark was very interested in the SVF partnership with Strike for Vets, since he is so passionate about bowling, and suggests that he wouldn't be the only veteran who would love to incorporate more competitive and athletic events into their social calendars. While recognizing that there are a number of ways to bring vets together to network and enjoy one another's company, Mark also recognizes that there's a particular type of environment and psychology around sports that resonates well with the veteran community.

"But there's no need for one veteran organization to compete with the other," he said. "Fill in the gaps of one another. Work together, and press on."

Chapter 7—Tapping into the Untapped Resources

S VF is dedicated to tapping into the resources in our student veterans that are so far overlooked or under-supported. We believe there's simply too much potential to waste. Because of our mission and my passion, the SVF vision incorporates many ideas that take advantage of the most sophisticated and successful strategies of advocacy groups.[51] We are here to stay, and I have many ideas on how to help veterans achieve more during their educational years.[52]

Helping Vets Navigate College Easily

One of the most challenging things that veterans struggle with on campus is the simple, disorganized bureaucracy. As every college freshman realizes, the campus is a large, often messy place, where people in different buildings are highly specialized in their areas and may not know much about the rest of how the school works.[53] Different colleges at the same university can have different requirements, and while the student may have completed his or her paperwork with one department, there may be another department he or she was not even aware of, but to which they are expected to report. It can be frustrating to run back and forth across campus to handle registration paperwork, financial aid requirements, and submit details to multiple offices around the school.

Of course, while every new student has to jump through a number of hoops to get their school year aligned and ready to proceed, veterans have a number of additional and special requirements in order to process all their G.I. Bill, housing requirements, or VA medical benefits. This is doubly difficult if they are disabled and require any reasonable accommodations to attend classes, in accordance with the Americans with Disabilities Act (ADA).[54] A truly successful student veteran organization should have services that help veterans navigate these frustrating bureaucratic waters.

Fortunately, some schools have started to recognize this. There are even a few who are working to combat this and bring veterans together in a more productive way by offering customized seminars that are only open for veterans to enroll in, like the one that Mark Singleton is enrolled in. These accredited and classroom-based, but optional, seminars guide them through the integration program, helping them adjust to the classroom; however, these orientation seminars are not offered at all schools, nor are they required for all former service members. At SVF, we believe they should be available on every campus, as well as a specialty veteran liaison who assists veterans one-on-one every day of the week.

RECOGNIZING VETERANS' LEADERSHIP

Student veterans are an untapped reserve of training, education, and leadership skills. SVF is dedicated to recognizing veterans for their leadership within their group, among their student colleagues, and within the larger community as a whole. While some colleges are beginning to tie together the fact that veterans are natural leaders who should be given more prominent positions at their schools, many are not. At SVF, we believe in shining the spotlight on those who deserve it most, including both the veterans on college campuses and the campuses that support them best.

There are some encouraging steps in the right direction. Some college campuses are beginning to award credit hours to student veterans who have been honorably discharged—providing them credit toward their education that doesn't require more work and dedication but, instead, recognizes the sacrifices that they have already made.

It's encouraging to see our universities begin to realize that this real-world experience should be rewarded, and be credited, toward the challenges veterans face at college. Perhaps some veterans are placed in positions where other students can see their success, but it is not enough to make a notable difference in the majority of college students' experience. We want to change that.

THE FINANCIAL ASSISTANCE & GUIDANCE VETERANS DESERVE

It's a well-known fact that, if you earn a college degree, you can earn more than twice the income over your lifetime than if you'd only earned a high school diploma. On top of that, if you earn a graduate or an advanced degree, you can earn more than ten times as much. Veterans come from all educational backgrounds and, without strong assistance to guide them through to their financial future, they can get lost.

While the G.I. Bill provides the benefits needed to keep students enrolled, it doesn't provide the coverage for all student veterans to clear their expenses.[55] While the needs of each campus' student veteran population varies, there are a few basics we know of that cost student veterans money, and with which SVF can help:

✓ **Accessible healthcare:** Veterans may have the medical

coverage and benefits, without the facilities or easily-accessible resources on campus. By providing them guidance on automated prescription refills that can be delivered, confirming they have access to the mental and physical healthcare facilities on campus, and working with them and their doctors if they need to go off-campus, veterans will save money by taking care of their most basic healthcare needs more efficiently.

✓ **Affordable childcare:** Many veterans have children, and many college campuses have affordable daycare for students, but many of these on-campus daycares don't offer preference for veterans or additional military discounts. In addition, many childcare services available near college campuses might offer discounts to veterans, but the veterans aren't aware which ones do. By providing student veterans with options for affordable childcare, SVF aims to help them save time and money with convenient childcare.

✓ **Financial advice & planning:** Everyone needs to know how to manage their money, set up a budget, create a savings plan, understand and procure life insurance, and a number of other basic financial services. Many veterans want to purchase a house or already own one, and they might be eligible to refinance with a VA loan or a special loan offered only to alumni of the school. By providing student veterans with access to tools and resources they can use to learn financial literacy, we will help them keep and enjoy the money they earn throughout their lives.

✓ **Book exchange, rental or swap services:** College textbooks are expensive, and classes that have labs or technological aids often include extra fees. Of course, college campuses have libraries, but they may not have the most recent editions of all books available, or the book the student needs may be checked out. SVF aims to help every student veteran to always have access to the required educational materials for their courses— whether that is through a book exchange or book swap program, by connecting student veterans who are using the same materials so they can share and work together, or providing whatever assistance we can to ensure that the cost of materials doesn't prevent them from succeeding.

I believe that no one should have to get "stuck" in a job. You should never be content to find a place in the working world that is content to buy off your dreams with a paycheck. Many people get into a job they don't love, thinking they'll only compromise for a year or two, but then it becomes ten years before they know it. And no one deserves that. No one deserves to spend their life treading water.

Long-Term Effects

There's no question that, when student veterans are better supported throughout their college careers, they will become more valuable assets to society in the long run. When veterans are provided the opportunities to demonstrate their servant leadership, they will act, and they will have impact. I believe that supporting student veterans' financial success while they're in school will have a ripple effect throughout decades and generations. When our veterans succeed, we all succeed. I believe that life is not about collecting things—it's about doing great things—and veterans who are financially supported during their education will do great things every day afterward.

CHAPTER 8—REVERSING THE ISOLATION THAT VETS FEEL

One of the best ways veterans can feel more at home and less isolated among their peers is to increase other students' education about what veterans go through. Creating a sense of community and a connection of a group of individuals with similar experiences reverses the isolation that can be so devastating. Connection helps veterans feel more engaged with the education process overall. Outreach programs can do an excellent job on campus of calling attention to the sacrifice military service members make, and the benefits of their experiences. By promoting education, you promote connection. Many students have a "video-game perspective" of leadership and teamwork but, by teaching them how the intellectual military tactics they are familiar with are connected with real-life experiences, you can increase empathy in non-veteran and veteran students alike.[56]

Veterans live among all of us in each of our communities. You probably saw one at the gas station this morning or the grocery store last weekend. While military life is a very normal experience for millions of men and women across the country, veteran life is not normalized.

Sometimes, the general public sees veterans as "strange" or "different" because of their experiences. People have heard about "shell shock" and the "horrors of war" all their lives and, although post-traumatic stress disorder (PTSD) is being more often addressed and better understood by many people, it also remains a frightening mystery to many. There are a lot of misunderstandings about what living with its symptoms is really like, not only among college students, but among older and more experienced adults as well.

SVF considers it important to remember that the larger community needs to see veterans and recognize them in order to see them as normal. To normalize the experience of living as a veteran, we have to show who veterans really are. Depictions of veterans from Hollywood and on TV can often show them as deeply damaged or even "broken" people. They are not broken.[57] They are strong, capable people with a lot of potential; they are the future leaders of our country.

BUILDING VETERANS' HOPES & DREAMS

Action-oriented people know how to put together a plan. They are forward thinking and they value results; however, often they are so busy *doing* that they don't *reflect* on their actions as much as they should, or they may not nurture their creativity or spirituality. In short, a plan is the "how to" of a dream but, if some people aren't given time to dream, whose plans are they putting into action?

A soldier is trained to take orders and, in the military, your individual plan is nowhere near as significant as the larger plan of the operation. In the military, your plan must align with the plan of the group, and "your" plan is never really your own. After military life, many veterans align their new plans with the idea of who they used to be before the military, or they align their plans with the needs of their current family. However, college is an environment where many people are learning to pursue their own dreams, and our veterans should have the services available to fully explore what their plans are for themselves.

I believe that, if you think about it, others have many plans for each of us, but no one else's plan is right for you but yours. If anyone lets someone else write his or her plan for them, the plan won't be as thorough or as satisfying when it's enacted. Anyone else's plan for you will be incomplete. The instructions won't be as clear or resonate with you in the same way as if you helped write them but, if you write your own plan, you make it from your own dreams, which come from within. Align your plan with a genuine understanding of who you are, and you'll find a true passion you can pursue all your life.

With this in mind, I believe that SVF should help connect every veteran with his or her genuine dream. Chapters can offer experiential services, letting veterans try out different career options or unique learning opportunities. I believe we should offer veterans job guidance and career coaching, helping them understand what profession will bring them long-term satisfaction, and what steps they should take in college to put themselves on that career path.

I also believe that we should help student veterans connect with the spiritual and religious services offered at their campus. Many campuses have representatives of numerous religious denominations, with chaplains who can advise student veterans seeking advice with finding their life's purpose. Many campuses also offer classes in meditation, yoga, Zen gardening, and a variety of other relaxation and spiritually enhancing practices that can help veterans relieve stress and find community, in addition to helping them connect with their inner voices about their passions, their hopes, and their dreams.

Without having to sign up for a semester-long class, student veterans should have the ability to try their hand at painting, dancing, creative writing, or digital game design—any type of creative endeavor that they could use to enhance their profession or excite their personal passions. Veterans should have the chance to volunteer, to work with children, and to be members of a stage performance if they want. At SVF, we work to provide engaging events and supportive services that remain as uniform as possible across all campuses. We want to provide that helping hand to guide veterans from their first day on campus to their graduation and beyond. We believe that veterans should have the same chances to explore and find their passions in places they didn't expect. The world wants passion. The world of tomorrow will build on the passion of today's dreamers.

CONNECTION WITH JOB POTENTIAL

One of the best ways to get veterans engaged in the community is to help them find the right kind of employment. Not just a short-term internship or "job" during their school years—some place where they can work to build up someone else's business or help them execute some executive's dream—but, instead, satisfying, long-term career options. Colleges are built to help people become employable, so it should be part of the school's duty to give their students as many opportunities to pursue employment as possible.

Most college campuses host multiple "job fairs" or "career fairs" every year. Some host more than one per semester or even as many as one per month; however, how many of these opportunities are deeply connected with veterans or dedicated to hiring veterans? Of course, it depends on the specifics of the school but, often, there won't even be a military recruitment booth at the job fair, let alone a business that specifically is looking to hire veterans.

Research shows that veterans are drawn to businesses that advertise themselves as "veteran-friendly" in their hiring process. When seeking long-term careers, veterans look for other vets to connect with. When surveyed, 75% of veterans report that they are looking for a company with a track record of hiring veterans, and their evaluation of the company begins before the interview, then continues when they meet their first representative of the company Veterans pay attention to whether the person interviewing them is a veteran or mentions anything about veterans during the interview, and six out of ten (60%) of veterans are looking for a company with a special veteran onboarding program or veteran employee support group.[58]

What's the number of businesses that offer this kind of veteran-specific onboarding?[59] The numbers are hard to pin down. It seems like it could be as low as 10% of companies that offer a specific onboarding program for veterans. While this may be changing, as the military offers a checklist that employers can use to onboard veterans and more news coverage is being given to the fact that veterans have specific onboarding concerns, it continues to be an issue for most veterans today.

One of the only ways that this will change in the future is if more veterans become entrepreneurs. More business owners who have served in the military means more businesses involved in normalizing veterans throughout the community. SVF is dedicated to helping veterans find a company to work for that can bring them more personal satisfaction, while also utilizing their years of skills as training, or to help them build a business that fills the need in their community for veteran-owned businesses.

CHAPTER 9—THE SVF COMMUNITY

The goal of the Student Veterans Foundation (SVF) is to build a true community for all student veterans. We want there to be a place—both a physical and emotional place—on every college campus for veterans to go. We want veterans in every stage of life, from any background, to find a home during their education. The purpose and mission that SVF always keeps in mind is to get veterans engaged and active on our college campuses because we at SVF firmly believe that veteran engagement is important for the future leadership of the U.S.

At SVF, we believe the only way to fully support veterans to the level they deserve is by adding a value-centered program with benefits that are both internal (within the school) and external (outside the school). The program should offer benefits that directly benefit student veterans and their families; it is vital to the success of every student veteran. It's not that there isn't some support for veterans and their dependents but, as we've seen, there are certainly opportunities to do more.

Through academic support, leadership opportunities, and engaging social events, the SVF community will create the spaces where veterans can connect. SVF aims to help connect all service members' military experience to their education, to connect their old life to their new one.[60] We are dedicated to helping them transfer the knowledge they gained during their service ultimately to civilian employment or entrepreneurship. We know that college is not "the end" for any student veteran, and we operate from a perspective that it's an honorable service to help all veterans get to their own ultimate end goals.

STUDENT VETERAN ACADEMIC SUPPORT

Ask most students why they chose to go to college, and they will tell you, "To get a degree." They might know the specific topics they want to focus on in their studies, but the bottom line for most is to become better educated in something. Student veterans are no different, and they deserve all the help they can get. They deserve tutoring and educational support services that will ultimately facilitate their careers and individual growth.

SVF aims to support all veterans in their academic process. A student veteran may need help with the updated technology available at the university; they may need tutoring in a specific subject they've never encountered before or haven't handled for a long time. Most students benefit from a study group or a focused reading group that allows them to hear other perspectives and join together to solve problems. And, while the non-veteran population has a ton of resources to help student veterans with this, a veteran-specific organization is needed. At SVF, we think each campus should provide customized academic resources for student veterans, providing them with reliable study groups and tutoring options.

In particular, many veterans do not know when they enroll in school that they might have a learning disability or be eligible for accommodation for physical or mental challenges they may be dealing with due to their service. Especially for disabled veterans, there are often cognitive or social results that they aren't aware of until they enter an educational environment. Once they become part of a student body, or once they begin to adjust their lives to accommodate any online or part-time education, they may discover they need extra help simply to maintain the pace at which the class runs through material.

Depending on their situations, disabled veterans, or those with special needs, might be eligible for extensions on class assignments, a revised syllabus, or technological accommodation. Students may be allowed to record class sessions for later review, have an assistant or note taker assigned to them, or even be assigned a specific seat in the classroom, based on their needs. Professors and instructors are required to provide reasonable accommodation for students with learning or cognitive processing issues, and our veterans need to know that and to have easy access to those vital educational resources.

SERVANT LEADERSHIP IN WORKING WITH VETERANS

As I have found out in my life, leadership makes a real difference. Through the embarrassing list of cool things I've done, I've realized that awards and recognition are nice, but they're not my main purpose. They are not what drives me. I enjoy helping others, serving them through my leadership. I know that, if leading others by serving them helps me answer the call to the life I want to live, that there are others out there who hear the similar call, but who haven't had the opportunity to answer it.[61]

SVF is dedicated to helping veterans be selected for and successful in positions of leadership on campus. There are so many opportunities for veterans to be mentors, role models, speakers, tutors, leaders, and even teachers on college campuses, and we will make sure that veterans know those roles are available and, if they want them, they are given every opportunity to succeed. I believe that every person grows through leadership, and college is an essential place where our veterans should be provided every opportunity for growth.

Some graduate students are teachers' assistants and, on some campuses, they are given the opportunity to join the Teachers' Union. If a student veteran is working as a TA and wants a leadership role at their college's Teachers' Union, they deserve every chance to obtain that role. They deserve the same opportunities as any other Union member. We want to help them.

On some campuses, veterans are a valuable resource for the ROTC program or recruitment offices on campus or near campus—and there's generally one for each branch near a major college campus. Veterans can be utilized to help recruits prepare for their enlistment, answer questions, lead seminars, or otherwise be involved with helping new service members with their transition into military life, but this connectivity is not built into every campus or available for every veteran. We want to build on this natural relationship.

And these are just two examples. There are dozens of more ways that veterans can be provided with more and better opportunities to be mentors and publicly acknowledged for it. Leadership and mentor roles like this often go unnoticed by most others on campus, and even more by the community at large. Because we're proud of the heroes we serve at SVF, we want to change that. We want to make celebration and commendation of our veterans more than ceremonial—we want it to be impressive. We want every college campus to celebrate veterans like we celebrate the Fourth of July.

STUDENT VETERANS' SPORTS GROUPS

Many of today's veterans are used to being physically active. Whether they were involved in sports before their enlistment—which a high percentage of them were—they certainly became used to physical activity during their service. If there's one thing you can say about most veterans—they don't tend to be lazy or inactive.

Research has long shown the impact that physical activity, exercise, and athleticism can have on a person's physical and mental wellbeing. When someone is engaged in a regular workout routine, especially a social one that combines physical activity with an engaging social setting, they are far more likely to relieve stress, feel connected to others, and boost their overall mentality to achieve more success in their lives.

One of the core ways that SVF wants to engage with veterans is through physical activity—after all, we got started as Strike for Vets, which brought together people to go bowling and raise money for veterans, and we're continuing that with sports like baseball and softball on an organizational level. Wherever we'll be striking for vets, we'll be working to bring benefits to more student veterans.

On a chapter level, each SVF chapter will be provided with the tools it needs to meet the unique engagement requirements of their members. Maybe the members want to form a workout group and need a trainer to help lead them through a course. Maybe the members want to co-ordinate a monthly group run or softball game and need a private social media group to get everyone on the same page. Whatever the need is, SVF will be there to help student veterans get together to enjoy camaraderie in fun, physically challenging ways that support their mental wellbeing, just as much as their educational success.

A SHARED VISION

For SVF, I envision building a community with a unified mission at every college campus, driven by a shared vision. While each SVF branch should, and will, adjust to the specific needs of the veterans in their study body, there is an underlying emotional push at the heart of every SVF branch. Underneath it all is servant leadership. We want to lead veterans to success by serving them, and we want them to continue to lead and serve others on their path to success. Whether it's through educational, social, or emotional support, we will be there to serve.

Chapter 10—With Honor and Gratitude

Who is Daniel Bolan?

My parents adopted me from an orphanage in Romania when I was two years old. My entire life, I had nagging doubts about whether I fit in. I even wondered if my name was the right name, or if I was bound to a destiny that was determined by my birth parents or one that was determined by my adoptive parents.

Raised in the Presbyterian church, I also worked hard to earn a black belt in Tae Kwon Do and a purple belt in Kung Fu. Early in my life, I decided that what I did wouldn't be a reflection of some destiny handed down by family—it would come from within. It would be my own legacy. I became an Eagle Scout and was recognized in my community as a leader. For my Eagle project, my group raised more than $50,000 and gave a drug-ridden area in central Florida new life as a memorial garden that honored those killed in senseless acts of violence. I made up my mind that I wouldn't let challenges be excuses for failure. I decided, in some vague and childish way, that I wasn't going to let other people place limits and labels on me.

In college, I'll be busy. I plan to double-major in Internal Affairs and Russian, and I plan to go on to pursue a Juris Doctorate (law degree) after my undergraduate studies. I have big goals for how I can help veterans of foreign wars and international campaigns, as well as the men and women who serve in civil positions with the CIA and other intelligence agencies. Their work is important, as impactful as military service members, and often overlooked in terms of follow-up and reintegration services.

From an early age, I've learned that there are few real limitations. Sometimes, people are truly limited by physical, mental, or emotional disabilities. Those people truly deserve compassion; those people truly deserve the help of people who can afford to help them. I've met people who live with conditions that are so severe that other people would use the word "handicapped," but those people never describe themselves that way. They overcome everything. I have met people in wheelchairs who are in better health and stronger than most able-bodied people. I've learned that, more often than not, what people call limitations are excuses and objections; however, now I know that, with determination, a person who is challenged can overcome anything.

STUDENT VETERANS FOUNDATION IS SOMETHING DIFFERENT

I began developing the idea for the Student Veterans Foundation over five years ago, when I was just 14 years old. When I was younger, I was a champion bowler, and I remain one today. In 2019, I am the FSHAA State Champion, National Team Champion, and a member of Team Romania.

Although I enjoyed the sport for its own sake when I was a kid, I began to find myself involved in more and more charity events, which I absolutely loved. The feeling of using my talent to do good for a group of worthy people really warms my heart. I began attending events as a representative of different local veterans' associations, and I developed a bit of a reputation for always partnering with organizations that support vets. Then, a friend of my family developed the "iCam bowler," which was a bowling ball apparatus that allowed people in wheelchairs to enjoy bowling. It was just natural to me to introduce this to the veterans I knew who were living in wheelchairs.

Along with my dad's inspiration and guidance, I came to realize I didn't have to be the spokesperson for someone else's organization. I could start an organization of my own, and so my first charity organization, "Strike for Vets," was born. After my Eagle Scouts project, I wanted to share the feeling of gratitude and joy I felt from giving back. I wanted to get more people involved, so I organized a group of students at my high school. We started Strike for Vets, combining our passion for bowling with our mission to help wounded warriors.

With Strike for Vets, we began raising funding and awareness for paralyzed veterans, helping to rebuild a rehab center in Tampa over six years. Together, we provided different services to help various veterans' charities, in honor of all those we knew in our own lives who had served. We began a national tour with a youth movement that helped local and national organizations like Fisher House. We also began attending more and more events, handing out specialized Strike for Vets bowling balls and customized swag to veterans who attended, watching the smiles spread across their faces as I could help bring a small moment of joy to their lives.

Now, I have grown this model and Strike for Vets operates as the events branch of the Student Veterans Foundation. It began with Strike for Vets, and it's grown. What began with a simple sponsored event has grown into an entire program that is aimed to spread nationwide and cause ripples on college campuses across the country. We have taken Strike to Vets to the next level by beginning to involve professional softball and baseball. It makes my heart swell to see how much bigger my dream is growing.

THE MESSAGE OF SVF

The successes I've had at such a young age are not entirely thanks to my own efforts. I had great parents, coaches, and opportunities but, more than anything, I was lucky enough to discover my own reason for being, my own unique purpose, early in my life. That is what I want to help others do. I understand that the student veterans I connect with have already found a purpose and mission for one stage of their lives, and have charted a clear course for the next goal, and I believe they deserve more than just a pat on the back and my best well-wishes.

The message of SVF is that each veteran deserves the utmost respect and honor for their service and sacrifice. I strive to live my life to do everything with honor and thanks, especially for our country's veterans, because they deserve more. Each of us is here for our own reason. We have our own desires, but we must learn to use our determination and discipline to grab hold of the opportunities and turn dreams into reality.

I strongly believe that veterans are the right people to provide the leadership that college campuses need. As I enter college and begin on the next chapter of my life, I am reminded that I will have the opportunity to meet these real-life heroes in real life. I will smile and shake the hand of each. I will thank them for their service because my purpose is to serve others, to lead by serving others and, as I am able to fulfill this purpose, I will reap the rewards of watching others achieve their purposes, too.

Once you find your purpose, you'll see the opportunities that are presented to you that can help you achieve that purpose. Great opportunities are only seen by people who are prepared, people who are ready to take the opportunities presented to them.

CHAPTER 11—MAXIMUM MEMORY MASTERY

The Student Veterans Foundation has done extensive research into the needs of veterans on college campuses. In the research, not only do veterans need to be supported on campus but also off campus with their families and communities. In building our on-campus programs, we will consider veterans' personal growth as well as building skills that can applied with their families, work lives, and community activities. Thus, we have focused on designing an integrated program that benefits the full family unit, veterans' social contacts as well the veteran on campus.

In development of the curriculum, we learned that having an accredited program is vital to sustainability by providing skills that can be used in all parts of a veteran's life. We have considered the cultural changes that take place when a participant moves from a commanded and controlled environment to one where their own experiences, ideas, and creativity become the value they offer to their various networks. However, these skills may not be recognized in the unstructured collegiate environment, where professors and peers may not know someone is a veteran or has this level of experience.

The Student Veterans Foundation has collaborated with the people who have developed process innovation, leadership, creativity, teamwork and training to learn skills that are world class, used in corporate America for decades. They are documented in two books co-authored by Tony Dottino: *Grass Roots Leaders*[62] and *The BrainSmart Leader.*[63]

Tony Dottino, throughout a distinguished career at IBM, was the visionary behind process management.[64] Along with extensive work in this area, he was instrumental in development of the criteria of the Malcom Baldrige Award and the founder of the USA Memory Championship[65] that has been broadcast on every major TV network, as well as covered by the *NY Times*, *USA Today*, and *Wall Street Journal*. While at IBM, he received two highly prestigious awards, a President's Award for Innovation and Teaching Excellence and a Chairman's Award for Leadership Excellence.[66]

Multiple Fortune 500 companies are using the work of Mr. Dottino that include: IBM, Johnson & Johnson, UTI Global, J.P. Morgan, Department of Homeland Security, Con Edison, and Advent Health, as well as many other national and international organizations.

His son Michael recently left a management position after almost 20 years at the Disney Company and joined Tony to bring Learning to Learn, Memory Skills and the USA Memory Championship to Penn State and MIT for their twenty-second annual competition. In his early work with Tony, he created an amazing online course that is the subject of a federal grant, sponsored by MIT, Columbia, and Princeton Neuroscience: Maximum Memory Mastery.[67]

They have a core belief supported by years of experience and research: there is more that people can do to improve their own intelligence, creativity, leadership, learning and, most important, their lives, than they might ever think possible.

They have developed a series of courses—Leadership Frameworks™,

Developing Leaders Through Grass Roots Innovation (GRI), Memory Management (Learning to Learn)—that have made a large difference in how people from 12 to 70 go about living their lives by finding new pathways of hope.[68]

When you listen to them, you will hear a major concern: "Humans are outsourcing their brains to technology. What are the longer-term impacts to their mental and cognitive health?" Thus, their series of workshops provide alternatives that lead to raving fans who have learned how to create new possibilities in their day-to-day living.

Their passion for helping veterans stems from their long-term commitment to helping people who serve others, which includes a variety of service industries, i.e., hospitals, hotels, and veterans.

They offer the answers to questions such as,

1) How do you communicate your intentions in an effective way to get the desired outcome from it?

2) What happens to a veteran who has led a life of where everything is planned for each hour of a day to creating their own priorities and value?

3) What leadership skills exist in a non-military world that help to influence and impact others that will lead to trusting relationships?

4) Can they be taught how to receive feedback that is constructive to their goals and leads to success, thus maximizing their value to a public that questions their service?

5) How can they create a clear goal/vision followed by appropriate actions?

6) What is a process of thinking that leads to 'Yes, I can'?

These are just a sampling of questions they raise for discussion with solutions throughout their workshops, and those discussions often lead to successes their students always wanted but needed support and pathways/skills to reach.

Research, as recent as January 2020, reported on *Neuroscience News*, reveals we have newly identified potentials that give humans unique brain power, which helps us solve computational problems.[69] In our program, it becomes a crucial starting point to get veterans to have a total comprehension of the potential that each of them possesses. This is followed by a "so what?" class discussion as to what this can mean to each participant. It's a goal to get each person to reflect on their own infinite powers to create new thinking and possibilities.

When Tony first began his research to this point, he was inspired by learning that, over the next 20 years, we would learn things about our own knowledge about our brain that would be proven wrong. He became curious as to what research would reveal as technology improved to the point where research could be done while people were alive, rather than having to donate their brains to science once they passed.

He thought of a hypothesis, "What if simply learning more about how your brain works could help you grow in both your personal and professional life?" He would introduce people to Play-Doh and ask them to sculpt their brain and what they thought of it.

Wow, what a difference it began to make in how people rethought about their own mental capacities. Can veterans go through a similar exercise to create a different mold of their own brains and their possibilities?

Research continued to reveal amazing results about human capacity, and this led to his founding of the USA Memory Championship in 1997 to demonstrate to people that something most people fear, losing their memory, is not a foregone conclusion but one we can influence to some degree by engaging in mental challenges. Is it a possibility to create mental athletes' clubs in academia and have schools challenge schools?

The goal of all of this is to move anyone who needs support to leave the victim mentality and become a master of change, beginning with their own lives, then extended to their family members, followed to work associates, and then their social networks. Assignments in the workshops are designed to have each learning session be followed by practicing in each of these modalities.

As reports continue to surface, there are several findings that have been consistently reported about maintaining maximum cognitive function:

1) **Proper nutrition**, a field that continues to expand and reveal new lessons for proper eating. But, for now, what's good for the heart is good for the brain. Some studies have shown that vitamins are not the way to go. Do people think taking a pill or vitamin a day is all they need to do?

2) **Physical activity and exercise** is a major benefit to improved brain function since the brain uses 20% of the oxygen we have in our bodies for our thinking.[70] Are we becoming a passive society, laptops, sitting all day, watching TV at night? In their service, our veterans are active; what happens to this when they have work, families, community service…time for exercise?

3) **Mental challenges**. What are solid mental exercises? This has created tremendous interest in the USA Memory Championship to study mental athletes. There have been hundreds who have competed, and many have made wonderful changes in their lives.

4) **Social interactions**. We are hard wired for being part of

teams, a network of people.[71] How do we welcome veterans back into their families, work units, and most important, into the academic community? What can they learn that facilitates this process?

5) **Stress**, processed too harshly in our brain, creates toxins within our bodies. See *Forgive to Live* by Dick Tibbits.[72] Since stress is something we all have, how do we build resilience to it, change our self-talk, and do something constructive?

6) **Sleep** to some minimum level is how our brain stores learning and re-sorts out the information that is important to retain and that which can exit. Though there are times we cannot sleep at night, which is not ideal, how do you handle those moments? Do something called a 'mind map' and get back to sleep.

Astute people, organizations and companies know that their future success depends on an intangible resource, the creativity of their human assets. This leads to a recognition that this is driven by stored knowledge and life experiences. Thus, the question arises: How do veterans utilize their amazing life stories to feed a creative process within the enterprises that may employ them? How can they take control of their own value and present it within their communities to become leaders in all aspects of their living that influence positive outcomes?

Through years of research, workshops for executive leaders, middle managers and front-line team members, studying the lives of the mental athletes in the USA Memory Championship for 21 years, collaborating with Penn State, MIT, and Princeton, we have developed a curriculum that is time-tested, with life-changing results. What has been most impactful is the participants in all of this have brought the skills taught into new ways of thinking that have led to new possibilities, people becoming the best they can be within themselves.

This has led to family relationships that grow stronger and our students becoming teachers to their family members. What a difference in these relationships, work colleagues, and social communities.

In our next chapter, we will take you through some of the most powerful teaching segments and how they impact lives!

Chapter 12—What is the Curriculum? Where do we start?

Mind Mapping

Mapping each person's mind through the use of Mind Mapping. Think of the brain as the trunk of a tree and mapping out all the branches of thoughts and emotions that are present on a given topic connected in an internodal series of thinking.

Through all the work that Tony and Michael have done, they have found that teaching people how to mind map is the first skill that provides the quickest and most impactful way of getting a conversation going that reflects on existing thoughts and feelings that one brings to the table. It represents their history book of experiences and how present it may be in their minds at a point in time. More important, it is a skill that helps them improve their learning, creativity, and communications—writing, speaking, listening and retention (memory) of valuable information.

Next: how do they build their own self-confidence in such a compelling demonstration of themselves that puts them on the pathway to success?

Think of it as mapping a mind and learning where people are in their state of thought and emotions.

Ask each veteran to begin by mapping out:

A) What branch of service were you in?

B) Why did you select that division?

C) What were your best experiences from it?

D) How might these be used to enhance your post-military life?

A map with this information could provide immediate guidance to the best approach to take with their growth and value to their social groups. Over time, it grows new branches and provides a personal vision with a laser focus of where they are going: HOPE for a better tomorrow.

This is followed by having each veteran map:

A) Why did you enroll in a college program?

B) What have you enjoyed most about it?

C) How has your military experience helped you?

D) What are some of obstacles that get in your way of being the best you can be?

FINDING YOUR LEARNING BUDDIES/TEAM

We do an exercise in the teaching of Mind Maps that asks them to map out what makes them happy. We then have them share this exercise in the classroom, at home, and on social networks, and look to find people who laugh, have fun together and, thus, find a road to uncovering new relationships and ways of enhancing existing relationships. The net focus is to create teams of people who support one another in the goals they have set for themselves.

We have utilized this approach in schools ("Learning Buddies") in sales teams (thus creating "Selling Buddies"), and at work (creating "Can do Teams"). In all cases, the power of two to five people working together has always outperformed those working alone. So why do we leave our veterans with feelings of loneliness, depression, and a lost sense of hope?

This will make a huge difference! Help them build social skills that teach them in simple ways how to build stronger relationships and strong support teams.

THE MOST FREQUENTLY ASKED QUESTION

In more than twenty years of work utilizing this tool, the most frequently asked question is, "Why haven't I been taught this before?"

This skill that a veteran learns at college and brings to the family has proven over and over to change the socialization of the family and help kids improve their learning in school.

Since this tool sets the foundation for bringing information into a brain, then helps to create comprehension, stores it for long-term use, and facilitates recall, it has numerous uses that help in all aspects of life. The secret sauce is knowing when to put the tool to use, and thus it is used throughout each course we offer to veterans.

In the Maximum Memory Mastery program (M3), we provide the basics of the tool and how to bring it to use within the family. In the Leadership Frameworks course, it is used to help leaders set vision, create goals, define roles, and identify strategies. And, in the GRI workshop, it is used to identify root causes of problems, bring creativity into play in developing powerful action plans, and communicating urgency to getting things done.

WHAT ARE TIPS FOR MEMORY AND CREATIVITY?

As the M3 course is the first stage of learning, as defined by inputting information, comprehending it, and processing it for use, it sets the foundation of memory and creativity. Skills are used in every conversation we have with every person, leading to seeing experiences with a brand-new lens.

Part of the Memory Management curriculum that seems so basic but captures focus and use begins with sharing the science of how many potential thoughts, ideas, and creative pathways we can generate. As one former veteran student exclaimed, "You have taught me how to think, not just do. Wow!"

Combining seven tips of memory with mind mapping gets students enthused and believing in themselves. What are these seven tips, and do they make sense? We are often asked, "Why aren't we taught these skills in school?"

1) You have to **remember to remember**. When listening to a lecture or reading a book, the time to think about how to retain the information is before you even attend the lecture or pick up the book. You have to ask yourself, "What skills/systems of learning/memory should I use before the information comes into my brain?" We are often told, "I have just read a chapter for a test I have tomorrow, and I cannot remember it." We will ask, "Did you think about how you were going to input it to your brain before you read it?" Next time you park your car, make sure you are focused in that moment to take fifteen seconds to anchor the location of where it is by finding a stationary object and using it to find your car when you look for it.

2) Your brain is like a muscle, **use it or lose it**. What are you doing to exercise your brain?

3) Your brain has 100 billion neurons, providing the foundation for infinite creativity and **capacity for learning**.

4) The **more you learn, the easier it becomes to learn** more, no matter what your age.

5) **Stress is a memory killer.** What are you doing to recognize your stress, its triggers, and how to build resilience?

6) Memory is a skill that can be improved **at any age**. The hardest part we have discovered is getting people to realize this is true. To see for yourself, visit the USA Memory Championship web site (www.usamemorychampionship.com) and Facebook page (watch the Live with Tony series of livestreams).

7) **Master memory rhythms** (periodic review). This is the process that moves items from short-term to long-term memory. Most people don't realize that, unless they periodically review material, 80% of what they learn is forgotten within one week![73]

These are the opening modules of our Maximum Memory Mastery workshop that build excitement, energy and enthusiasm to build on success and grow bigger trees.

WHAT ELSE IS IN M3?

These modules are followed by a series of memory systems and lessons that lead to remembering the names and faces of people you meet, especially those you meet again. It has been said by many people, "I can't believe he/she remembered my name and a few things about me." The more you learn about someone, the easier it becomes to remember it.

If reading is crucial, there are lessons about how to improve your reading speed while improving your comprehension. Sounds too good to be true, doesn't it? Yet, the science shows that proper speed-reading techniques improve speed and comprehension. These lessons begin to integrate various components of the M3 course into day-to-day learning from the classroom or during post-class assignments.

Is it also important to remember numbers. This is true for addresses, zip codes, serial numbers, and even phone numbers. If you don't think it is important to remember a phone number, you've never had to call someone when your cell phone battery was dead.

Throughout this course, there is a continuum of work assignments that can be applied to students' other classes, then to family, and eventually to work life and social communities. Our focus is to create innate learning skills while building self-confidence that leads to each student becoming the best of his or her own self. We recommend creating Mental Athlete Clubs on each campus and having a Memory Competition among college teams.

There are numerous life lessons in the M3 online course, and it even includes bonus materials that people love (e.g., memorizing a deck of playing cards, using memory techniques to give a presentation).

If anyone wants to purchase this course, go to www.maximummemorymastery.com and, as a reader of this book, enter discount code **SVF15** for a 15% discount.

WHAT COMES NEXT?

In building a life-changing pathway for people, an assessment of their present position in life, along with their maps of their vision and goals, decides which course comes next in their learning.

Let's go through each and realize that all three of these courses are integrative and lead to major positive changes in living life. With the support networks from it, add to it trusting people who will be there to help you reach your goals/success.

In Tony's years of research of the human brain, he began to uncover things that every leader needs to know in order to engage and inspire the creativity of their workforce. His initial book, *BrainSmart Leader,* was published in more than 12 countries and written for a mid-level to executive management audience. After this success, his publisher asked if he could co-author a second book for front-line managers and developing new leaders, and this is *The Grass Roots Leader* book.

WHAT IS THE LEADERSHIP FRAMEWORKS COURSE?

The Grass Roots Leader has led to the creation of a workshop named "Leadership Frameworks" that has been used at various levels of leadership for more than ten years. A framework is defined as a foundation of thinking that, applied to every part of life and reflecting on it, will lead you to making the best decisions that provide the best possible outcomes.

This provides a semester for people wanting to learn how to improve their leadership skills and lead people in ways that build trust, buy-in to outcomes, create communications that are transparent, know when to lead through crisis versus being proactive, and how to transform a culture.

It has a series of 60- to 90-minute lessons that each require a series of practical applications that must be done as part of participating in this class. Significant learning takes place as the students share the results of their assignments with their fellow students.

The curriculum begins with a review of Mind Mapping, but now with a focus on how to utilize it to set a clear direction, build a vision and set of goals, identify strategies, establish roles, and identify who is on the team and working toward the mission with the total use of their infinite creative brain.

WHAT IS GIGG?

Within this is a section that continues to build on the lessons applied from the initial class from Maximum Memory Mastery. It is called "GIGG." The brain has a unique ability of synergy to build on its own thinking. Try not thinking for five seconds and see if you can do it. In fact, your brain is in action 24/7/365. But what direction does it move within itself, and what inputs influence its direction?

Thus, garbage input to a brain will result in Garbage Growing that will equal negative thinking and possibly depression by keeping it engaged with this model day after day. The brain builds a garbage dump that begins to reek and discourage us from trying anything new or hoping for a better life. We can call this "negative thinking," "pessimism," "cynicism," and it just continues to breed more of the same.

Well, because humans have the ability to influence their own GIGG, we have the option of changing the two Gs into "Good In" and "Good will Grow." Even better, we have found bold and audacious people who change this G into GREATNESS in and GREATNESS WILL GROW, thus creating their own life's success.

The key is: How do you begin to move from one G to the next? As part of the GIGG lesson, there is an initial assignment given. Go home that evening and have a five-minute conversation in person or on phone with a family memory, spouse, child, mother, father, neighbor, cat, dog, and ask them what were three good things that happened during their day.

The goal is to begin each interaction with people with the good things going on in their lives, which begins to create a much more welcoming dialogue once it becomes routine. Does it work easily on the first few tries? Not if people are so used to talking about the day's misery. Just watch the evening news for an example of this.

Tony remembers talking to a TV producer, suggesting they start a broadcast with the day's goodness. He was shocked at the response he got. "We have tried that on several pilots, and what we found is no one wanted to keep listening." And this is the culture we bring about us every day. In a conversation I had with Daniel's dad, I asked him, "What environment was this amazing young man brought into?" His dad responded, "I have always focused on who he associates with and how it influenced his life."

I believe that Daniel could become the president of the United States if he ever chooses politics. How great would that be?

Try this exercise in your own life. Begin the next conversation you have with someone by asking, "So what has brought a smile to your face today?" Or ask them to take a moment for a good thought. Make it your own and change the way you get to the good by being yourself. Make it natural.

When you ask veterans who and what are the five things that influence their current thinking, it uncovers a number of powerful insights that can help them move beyond anything they may have ever thought possible.

WHAT ELSE IS IN FRAMEWORKS?

We cover Brain To Brain Communication and the process of how we know that the intention of a communication will be carried out by the actions we expect to follow. Many an executive has said, "When you teach this as a class, it seems so simple, but when I go to apply it day to day, it is tough, but worth pursuing because of what you learn."

Following this are lessons of The Brain's Formula for Success and Why Feedback is the Lifeline to Success. How do you create an environment where people will have trust to give you the truth and thus build stronger relationships and high-powered teams?

We teach students the 7 Brain Principles every leader needs to be aware of if they are going to influence their teams to sustain the energy and enthusiasm that gets created.

We help identify the actions that lead us into a crisis and how to avoid them by becoming more proactive. There are exercises the veterans will go through that may lead to them redefining what a crisis is and what are characteristics of proactive leaders who wants to engage their front line.

Netting Out Leadership Frameworks

Leaders learn a set of skills that builds strong teams, loyal and committed to the organization's vision with their infinite creative brains figuring out the "how to" rather than the "why not." These skills can be applied in their family and community lives as well as their work lives.

The veterans who are enrolled in this program have a desire and passion to lead others and are willing to utilize their previous skills and add a few enhancements to it. They must comply with all required assignments and be willing to share the results of them with their classmates.

The third program is Developing Leaders through Grass Roots Innovation (GRI)

For veterans who want to become leaders and utilize their military experience to become valued members of their companies and organizations, this course will teach them how to build a megaphone that can be used to amplify their ideas and messaging to the managers/executives who provide the support to implement their ideas.

Background to this Course

Tony was heavily involved in the IBM quality efforts in the 1980s and had several major-quality gurus as his instructors. As he saw the value of these lessons and realized the impact the skills he was learning could make a huge difference in IBM's performance, he developed a series of skills and tools that would engage front-line people to fix their own problems.

In doing this, he defined a thoughtful process of putting the messaging together on where different levels of leadership needed to focus and taught this at the IBM Quality Institute. He became one of IBM's top instructors and got to refine this work over a number of years, to the point where he began to transition the managers of IBM not to think of their own departments but of a total process that addresses the end results of a string of departments, and how it eventually impacts the end user.

His work eventually got presented to a series of top executives, who then shared this with their major vendors and customers, and the outgrowth of this became Six Sigma.

He also had the opportunity of working with Dr. Jim Harrington, who was at IBM but also the president of the Quality Control Organization in California,[74] and helped Jim write the criteria for the Malcolm Baldrige Award.

LEAVING IBM AND FOUNDING DOTTINO CONSULTING GROUP

Tony left IBM in 1993 and started Dottino Consulting. He expanded the scope of his process improvement work by adding a level of neuroscience to his process skills. This has been used ever since as a workshop to engage front-line people in pitching their message with facts to whatever level of leadership needs to get behind making changes to how work gets done in their organizations.

THE ELEMENTS OF GRI

This workshop combines a simple level of process improvement principles:

1) What is a process?

2) What is an activity?

3) How would you distinguish between an activity and a task?

4) Who are the end users that define the requirements that must be met?

5) What are the required, preventative, appraisal, and failure tasks that make up the work in a process?

6) How do you get to a root cause, use a mind map, gather the metrics that will close the story, and lead to a compelling business case that demands urgency and corrective actions?

Upon leaving IBM, Tony discovered that, by adding a bit of neuroscience to this program, he could energize the creativity and excitement of people at the front line, who they wanted to become leaders, in making necessary changes to improving the value their organizations were providing to their clients.

WHO IS THIS FOR?

Any veteran who wants to learn how to speak in the boss' language and structure a conversation or presentation that is compelling and hits a bullseye will find this a huge benefit to the value they provide to their employer.

Numerous people who have taken this program over the last twenty years have become leaders, leading to very successful career paths.

In Tony's *Grass Roots Leader*, these are documented within the chapters. He has been given feedback over time that the curriculum in this book is used by professors teaching leadership and business classes, employees wanting to go back to higher education, and people who just want to find a way to improve their lives.

In collaboration with Daniel, Michael and Tony Dottino believe they can provide college class offerings that have been time-tested—supported by MIT, Princeton, and Columbia neuroscience departments—that will offer veterans new pathways of living a life that makes them the best they can be and creates an extension to their families, companies, and social networks.

It is best summarized by a call I had with a wife of a former student: "Thank you for giving me my Charley back, who in turn has helped my kids get through school that we never thought possible. Even getting him several promotions in his company, when I thought he was going to quit."

Conclusion

Share Our Message

Thank you, from the bottom of my heart, for spending your time with me discussing this issue. I can't tell you how much it means to me that you're interested and willing to support veterans across the country. I can't tell you how much it means that you're willing to listen.

Because I don't speak for myself, I have decided to use any platform that I can to trumpet the worthiest of causes—honoring those who have served you and, if I can reach more people to spread this message of love and honor, I can sleep happy every night.

I hope you have learned valuable information and have been given some interesting food for thought. I know I certainly was. I hope you have been able to see yourself, or someone you love, on these pages but, mostly, I hope you see how you can make a difference. You don't have to do much, but every effort counts, and every person's involvement helps us reach our goal.

If you are a veteran looking to connect with other veterans, I hope you will connect with us via the Student Veteran Foundation website or social media channels. Whether you are a student or not, we would love to have you as part of our community.

If you are not a veteran, look around you—you probably know a few! If any of them are students or are thinking of returning to school, I hope you'll share this book and its message. If you know a college student who is thinking about enlisting in the military, I hope you'll share this message with them and, if you look around you and know someone who is an administrator or involved in activities that go on at your local college's campus—please reach out to them. Ask them about what their school is doing to help veterans, and I hope you'll share with them the message and mission of SVF. The more people we know, the more good we can do.

Thank you again. Many blessings.

Daniel Bolan, SVF Founder and Board Member

September 2019

http://studentveteransfoundation.org/

ENDNOTES AND REFERENCES

1 "List of Presidents Who Were Veterans." 16 Feb. 2015. U.S. Department of Veterans Affairs Office of Veterans Health Administration. 17 Aug. 2019. https://www.va.gov/health/newsfeatures/2015/february/list-of-presidents-who-were-veterans.asp

2 "US Military Veterans' Difficult Transitions Back to Civilian Life and the VA's Response." Anna Zogas. Feb. 2017. Watson Institute: International & Public Affairs, Brown University. 17 Aug. 2019. https://watson.brown.edu/costsofwar/files/cow/imce/papers/2017/Zogas_Veterans%27%20Transitions_CoW_2.1.17.pdf

3 "U.S. active-duty military presence overseas is at its smallest in decades." Kristen Bialik. Pew Research Center. 22 Aug. 2017, Web article. 10 Aug. 2019. https://www.pewresearch.org/fact-tank/2017/08/22/u-s-active-duty-military-presence-overseas-is-at-its-smallest-in-decades/

4 "Navigating the College Experience." U.S. Department of Veterans Affairs Office of Research and Development. 26 Oct. 2017. "VA Research Currents: Research News from the U.S. Department of Veterans Affairs". 10 Aug. 2019. https://www.research.va.gov/currents/1017-Veterans-face-challenges-in-higher-education.cfm

5 "Navigating the College Experience." U.S. Department of Veterans Affairs Office of Research and Development. 26 Oct. 2017. "VA Research Currents: Research News from the U.S. Department of Veterans Affairs." 10 Aug. 2019. https://www.research.va.gov/currents/1017-Veterans-face-challenges-in-higher-education.cfm

6 "What to Do When the GI Bill Won't Cover College." Anna Helhoski. 22 May 2017. Blog. 10 Aug. 2019. https://www.nerdwallet.com/blog/loans/student-loans/veterans-pay-for-college-gi-bill/

7 "Veterans in Higher Education." Louis Hicks, Eugenia Weiss, & Jose Coll. *The Civilian Lives of U.S. Veterans: Issues and Identities.* Department of Veterans

Affairs. 2017. Google Book. 10 Aug. 2019. https://books.google.com/
books?id=43B1DQAAQBAJ&pg=PA155&lpg=PA155&dq=scandals+student+vete
rans+association&source=bl&ots=ZpVeErP0jf&sig=ACfU3U2UuMtQc9tA3uwoB
oHxxEx1kGBmdA&hl=en&sa=X&ved=2ahUKEwj_sfGQ04rkAhXoV98KHenSBa
I4ChDoATAHegQIBxAB#v=onepage&q&f=false

8 "Who Are Today's Student Veterans?" U.S. Department of Veterans Affairs VA
Campus Toolkit. ND. U.S. Department of Veterans Affairs. 10. Aug. 2019. https://
www.mentalhealth.va.gov/studentveteran/studentvets.asp

9 "Who Are Today's Student Veterans?" U.S. Department of Veterans Affairs VA
Campus Toolkit. ND. U.S. Department of Veterans Affairs. 10. Aug. 2019. https://
www.mentalhealth.va.gov/studentveteran/studentvets.asp

10 "Who Are Today's Student Veterans?" U.S. Department of Veterans Affairs VA
Campus Toolkit. ND. U.S. Department of Veterans Affairs. 10. Aug. 2019. https://
www.mentalhealth.va.gov/studentveteran/studentvets.asp

11 "Who Are Today's Student Veterans?" U.S. Department of Veterans Affairs VA
Campus Toolkit. ND. U.S. Department of Veterans Affairs. 10. Aug. 2019. https://
www.mentalhealth.va.gov/studentveteran/studentvets.asp

12 "Student Veterans/Service Members' Engagement in College and University Life
and Education." Young M. Kim & James S. Cole. American Council on Education.
Dec. 2013. PDF. 6 Sept. 2019. https://www.acenet.edu/news-room/Documents/
Student-Veterans-Service-Members-Engagement.pdf

13 "Who Are Today's Student Veterans?" U.S. Department of Veterans Affairs VA
Campus Toolkit. ND. U.S. Department of Veterans Affairs. 10. Aug. 2019. https://
www.mentalhealth.va.gov/studentveteran/studentvets.asp

14 "Demographics of the U.S. Military." George M. Reynolds and Amanda
Shendruk. 24 April 2018. Council on Foreign Relations. 12 Aug. 2019. https://www.
cfr.org/article/demographics-us-military

15 "Why Men Are the New College Minority." Jon Marcus. 8 Aug. 2017. The
Atlantic. 15 Aug. 2019. https://www.theatlantic.com/education/archive/2017/08/
why-men-are-the-new-college-minority/536103/

16 "Navigating the College Experience." U.S. Department of Veterans Affairs Office
of Research and Development. 26 Oct. 2017. "VA Research Currents: Research
News from the U.S. Department of Veterans Affairs." 10 Aug. 2019. https://www.
research.va.gov/currents/1017-Veterans-face-challenges-in-higher-education.cfm

17 "Veterans in Higher Education." Louis Hicks, Eugenia Weiss, & Jose Coll.
The Civilian Lives of U.S. Veterans: Issues and Identities. Department of Veterans
Affairs. 2017. Google Book. 10 Aug. 2019. https://books.google.com/

books?id=43B1DQAAQBAJ&pg=PA155&lpg=PA155&dq=scandals+student+vete
rans+association&source=bl&ots=ZpVeErP0jf&sig=ACfU3U2UuMtQc9tA3uwoB
oHxxEx1kGBmdA&hl=en&sa=X&ved=2ahUKEwj_sfGQ04rkAhXoV98KHenSBa
I4ChDoATAHegQIBxAB#v=onepage&q&f=false

18 "The 12 Best Job Industries for Veterans." Kat Boogaard. ND.
ZipRecruiter.com. 6 Sept. 2019. https://www.ziprecruiter.com/blog/
the-12-best-job-industries-for-veterans/

19 "Navigating the College Experience." U.S. Department of Veterans Affairs Office
of Research and Development. 26 Oct. 2017. "VA Research Currents: Research
News from the U.S. Department of Veterans Affairs". 10 Aug. 2019. https://www.
research.va.gov/currents/1017-Veterans-face-challenges-in-higher-education.cfm

20 "Veterans Returning to College Face Unique Challenges." St. Louis Post-
Dispatch. 2019. Military.com. 15 Aug. 2019. https://www.military.com/veteran-
jobs/career-advice/military-transition/veterans-in-college-face-challenges.html

21 "Navigating the College Experience." U.S. Department of Veterans Affairs Office
of Research and Development. 26 Oct. 2017. "VA Research Currents: Research
News from the U.S. Department of Veterans Affairs". 10 Aug. 2019. https://www.
research.va.gov/currents/1017-Veterans-face-challenges-in-higher-education.cfm

22 "Navigating the College Experience." U.S. Department of Veterans Affairs Office
of Research and Development. 26 Oct. 2017. "VA Research Currents: Research
News from the U.S. Department of Veterans Affairs". 10 Aug. 2019. https://www.
research.va.gov/currents/1017-Veterans-face-challenges-in-higher-education.cfm

23 "Navigating the College Experience." U.S. Department of Veterans Affairs Office
of Research and Development. 26 Oct. 2017. "VA Research Currents: Research
News from the U.S. Department of Veterans Affairs". 10 Aug. 2019. https://www.
research.va.gov/currents/1017-Veterans-face-challenges-in-higher-education.cfm

24 "An Army of One Carries a High Price." Diana Olick. 21 Oct. 2002. NBCNews.
com. 10 Aug. 2019. http://www.nbcnews.com/id/3072945/t/army-one-carries-high-
price/#.XVimf-hKhnJ

25 "Isn't the Average US Soldier Poorly Talented Compared to Others from Other
Countries Since the US Military Rely so Much on Fire Power, Technology and
Logistics?" Allen Bruce. 21 March 2018. Quora. 17 Aug. 2019. https://www.
quora.com/Isnt-the-average-US-soldier-poorly-talented-compared-to-others-from-
other-countries-since-the-US-military-rely-so-much-on-fire-power-technology-a-
nd-logistics

26 An Army of One Carries a High Price." Diana Olick. 21 Oct. 2002. NBCNews.
com. 10 Aug. 2019. http://www.nbcnews.com/id/3072945/t/army-one-carries-high-
price/#.XVimf-hKhnJ

27 "The Cost of a Military Person-Year: A Method for Computing Savings from Force Reductions." National Defense Research Institute. 2007. Rand.org 17 Sept. 2019. https://www.rand.org/content/dam/rand/pubs/monographs/2007/RAND_MG598.pdf

28 An Army of One Carries a High Price." Diana Olick. 21 Oct. 2002. NBCNews.com. 10 Aug. 2019. http://www.nbcnews.com/id/3072945/t/army-one-carries-high-price/#.XVimf-hKhnJ

29 "Veteran Jobs." Military.com. ND. 6 Sept. 2019. https://www.military.com/veteran-jobs

30 "The 12 Best Job Industries for Veterans." Kat Boogaard. ND. ZipRecruiter.com. 6 Sept. 2019. https://www.ziprecruiter.com/blog/the-12-best-job-industries-for-veterans/

31 "3 Industries that Love to Hire Veterans." Code Platoon. 11 Feb. 2018. Code Platoon. 6 Sept. 2019 https://www.codeplatoon.org/3-industries-that-love-to-hire-veterans/

32 "Nearly Half of Job Searches by Veterans Focus on Three Industries: Monster." Staffing Industry Analysis. 5 Nov. 2018. Staffing Industry Analysis. 6 Sept. 2019. https://www2.staffingindustry.com/site/Editorial/Daily-News/Nearly-half-of-job-searches-by-veterans-focus-on-three-industries-Monster-47988

33 "Nearly Half of Job Searches by Veterans Focus on Three Industries: Monster." Staffing Industry Analysis. 5 Nov. 2018. Staffing Industry Analysis. 6 Sept. 2019. https://www2.staffingindustry.com/site/Editorial/Daily-News/Nearly-half-of-job-searches-by-veterans-focus-on-three-industries-Monster-47988

34 "Nearly Half of Job Searches by Veterans Focus on Three Industries: Monster." Staffing Industry Analysis. 5 Nov. 2018. Staffing Industry Analysis. 6 Sept. 2019. https://www2.staffingindustry.com/site/Editorial/Daily-News/Nearly-half-of-job-searches-by-veterans-focus-on-three-industries-Monster-47988

35 "Opportunities for Leadership in College." Kelci Lynn Lucier. 5 Aug. 2019. ThoughtCo.com. 17 Aug. 2019. https://www.thoughtco.com/opportunities-for-leadership-in-college-793360

36 "The Whys and Hows of Shared Leadership in Higher Education." Elizabeth Holcombe and Adrianna Kezar. 10 May 2017. Higher Education Today, American Council for Education. 17 Aug. 2019. https://www.higheredtoday.org/2017/05/10/whys-hows-shared-leadership-higher-education/

37 "Pathways to the University Presidency." Jeffrey Selingo, Sonny Chheng and Cole Clark. 18 April 2017. Deloitte Insights. 17 Aug. 2019. https://www2.deloitte.

com/insights/us/en/industry/public-sector/college-presidency-higher-education-leadership.html

38 "Promoting Student Leadership on Campus – Creating a Culture of Engagement." Rosana G. Rodriguez and Abelardo Villarreal. May 2003. Intercultural Development Research Association. 17 Aug. 2019. https://www.idra.org/resource-center/promoting-student-leadership-on-campus/

39 "Student Veterans/Service Members' Engagement in College and University Life and Education." Young M. Kim & James S. Cole. American Council on Education. Dec. 2013. PDF. 6 Sept. 2019. https://www.acenet.edu/news-room/Documents/Student-Veterans-Service-Members-Engagement.pdf

40 "Veterans Returning to College Face Unique Challenges." St. Louis Post-Dispatch. 2019. Military.com. 15 Aug. 2019. https://www.military.com/veteran-jobs/career-advice/military-transition/veterans-in-college-face-challenges.html

41 "Veterans in Student Government: The Coastal Carolina University Experience." Denny C. Powers. 20 Feb. 2017. NASPA: Student Affairs Administrators in Higher Education. 10 Aug. 2019. https://www.naspa.org/constituent-groups/posts/veterans-in-student-government

42 "Veterans in Higher Education." Louis Hicks, Eugenia Weiss, & Jose Coll. *The Civilian Lives of U.S. Veterans: Issues and Identities.* Department of Veterans Affairs. 2017. Google Book. 10 Aug. 2019. https://books.google.com/books?id=43B1DQAAQBAJ&pg=PA155&lpg=PA155&dq=scandals+student+veterans+association&source=bl&ots=ZpVeErP0jf&sig=ACfU3U2UuMtQc9tA3uwoBoHxxEx1kGBmdA&hl=en&sa=X&ved=2ahUKEwj_stGQ04rkAhXoV98KHenSBa14ChDoATAHegQIBxAB#v=onepage&q&f=false

43 "Veterans Returning to College Face Unique Challenges." St. Louis Post-Dispatch. 2019. Military.com. 15 Aug. 2019. https://www.military.com/veteran-jobs/career-advice/military-transition/veterans-in-college-face-challenges.html

44 "Navigating the College Experience." U.S. Department of Veterans Affairs Office of Research and Development. 26 Oct. 2017. "VA Research Currents: Research News from the U.S. Department of Veterans Affairs". 10 Aug. 2019. https://www.research.va.gov/currents/1017-Veterans-face-challenges-in-higher-education.cfm

45 "About Us – Student Veterans of America." Student Veterans of America. 2019. https://studentveterans.org/aboutus

46 About Us – Student Veterans of America." Student Veterans of America. 2019. https://studentveterans.org/aboutus

47 "Student Veterans/Service Members' Engagement in College and University Life and Education." Young M. Kim & James S. Cole. American Council on Education. Dec. 2013. PDF. 6 Sept. 2019. https://www.acenet.edu/news-room/Documents/ Student-Veterans-Service-Members-Engagement.pdf

48 "Veterans' Groups Compete with Each Other, and Struggle with the V.A." Jennifer Steinhauer. *NY Times*. 4 Jan. 2019. Web page. 19 Sept. 2019. https://www. nytimes.com/2019/01/04/us/politics/veterans-service-organizations.html

49 "Veterans Returning to College Face Unique Challenges." St. Louis Post-Dispatch. 2019. Military.com. 15 Aug. 2019. https://www.military.com/veteran-jobs/career-advice/military-transition/veterans-in-college-face-challenges.html

50 "Veterans Returning to College Face Unique Challenges." St. Louis Post-Dispatch. 2019. Military.com. 15 Aug. 2019. https://www.military.com/veteran-jobs/career-advice/military-transition/veterans-in-college-face-challenges.html

51 "The 5 Building Blocks of Successful Advocacy." Jennifer Gmerek. 30 June 2015. NonprofitPro. 15 Aug. 2019. https://www.nonprofitpro.com/ post/5-building-blocks-successful-advocacy/all/

52 "Effective Advocacy 101: How to Bring About Change in Five Steps." Lucy Drescher. *The Guardian*. 12 Jan. 2016. Web page. 6 Sept. 2019. https://www. theguardian.com/global-development-professionals-network/2016/jan/12/ effective-advocacy-101-how-to-bring-about-change-in-five-steps

53 "Veterans Returning to College Face Unique Challenges." St. Louis Post-Dispatch. 2019. Military.com. 15 Aug. 2019. https://www.military.com/veteran-jobs/career-advice/military-transition/veterans-in-college-face-challenges.html

54 "What is the Americans with Disabilities Act (ADA)?" ADA National Network. Sept. 2019. ADATA.org. 6 Sept. 2019. https://adata.org/learn-about-ada

55 "What to Do When the GI Bill Won't Cover College." Anna Helhoski. 22 May 2017. Blog. 10 Aug. 2019. https://www.nerdwallet.com/blog/loans/student-loans/ veterans-pay-for-college-gi-bill/

56 "Navigating the College Experience." U.S. Department of Veterans Affairs Office of Research and Development. 26 Oct. 2017. "VA Research Currents: Research News from the U.S. Department of Veterans Affairs". 10 Aug. 2019. https://www. research.va.gov/currents/1017-Veterans-face-challenges-in-higher-education.cfm

57 "Navigating the College Experience." U.S. Department of Veterans Affairs Office of Research and Development. 26 Oct. 2017. "VA Research Currents: Research News from the U.S. Department of Veterans Affairs". 10 Aug. 2019. https://www. research.va.gov/currents/1017-Veterans-face-challenges-in-higher-education.cfm

58 "Nearly Half of Job Searches by Veterans Focus on Three Industries: Monster." Staffing Industry Analysis. 5 Nov. 2018. Staffing Industry Analysis. 6 Sept. 2019. https://www2.staffingindustry.com/site/Editorial/Daily-News/Nearly-half-of-job-searches-by-veterans-focus-on-three-industries-Monster-47988

59 "Building an Inclusive Onboarding Process for Military Veterans." H.V. MacArthur. *Forbes magazine*. 18 Sept. 2019. Web page. 23 Sept. 2019. https://www.forbes.com/sites/hvmacarthur/2019/09/18/building-an-inclusive-onboarding-process-for-military-veterans/#794ae23e2b55

60 "Now Hear This: The 9 Laws of Successful Advocacy Communications." Fenton Communications. Nae.edu. 2009. PDF. 16 Aug. 2019.

61 "Desire, Determination and Discipline." Daniel Bolan. 5 July 2019. MS Word. 17 Aug. 2019.

62 *Grass Roots Leaders: The BrainSmart Revolution in Business*. Tony Buzan, Tony Dottino, Richard Israel. Gower Publishing Company. 2007.

63 *The BrainSmart Leader*. Tony Buzan, Tony Dottino, Richard Israel. Gower Publishing Company. 1999.

64 "Tony Dottino." Dottino Consulting Group. 2020. Website page. 15 Jan. 2020. http://www.dottinoconsulting.com/?team=tony-dottino

65 "Accomplishments." Dottino Consulting Group. 2020. Website page. 15 Jan. 2020. http://www.dottinoconsulting.com/accomplishments/

66 "Tony Dottino." LinkedIn. 2020. Web profile. 15 Jan. 2020.

https://www.linkedin.com/in/tonydottino/

67 "Michael Dottino." Dottino Consulting Group. 2020. Website page. 15 Jan. 2020. http://www.dottinoconsulting.com/?team=michael-dottino

68 "Unleashing the Possibilities." Dottino Consulting Group. Jun. 2016. PDF. 15 Jan. 2020. http://www.dottinoconsulting.com/wp-content/uploads/2016/06/Dottino-Overview-Brochure.pdf

69 "Newly identified dendritic action potentials give humans unique brain power." Neuroscience News.com. 2 Jan. 2020. Website article. 15 Jan. 2020. https://neurosciencenews.com/dendritic-action-potential-15380/

70 "Study Reveals Brain's Finely Tuned System of Energy Supply." Mark Michaud. University of Rochester Medical Center. 8 Aug. 2016. Website article. 15 Jan. 2020. https://www.urmc.rochester.edu/news/story/4619/study-reveals-brains-finely-tuned-system-of-energy-supply.aspx

71 "Teamwork made humans brainier: study." AFP. ABC Science. 11 April 2012. Website article. 15 Jan. 2020. https://www.abc.net.au/science/articles/2012/04/11/3474794.htm

72 *Forgive to Live: How Forgiveness Can Save Your Life.* Dick Tibbits. Thomas Nelson Publishers. 5 Oct. 2008.

73 "Brain Science: The Forgetting Curve – the Dirty Secret of Corporate Training." Art Kohn. Learn Solutions. 13 March 2014. Website article. 15 Jan. 2020. https://learningsolutionsmag.com/articles/1379/brain-science-the-forgetting-curvethe-dirty-secret-of-corporate-training

74 "H. James Harrington." CRC Press: Taylor & Francis Group. 2020. Website page. 15 Jan. 2020. https://www.crcpress.com/authors/i76-h-james-harrington

www.ingramcontent.com/pod-product-compliance
Lightning Source LLC
Chambersburg PA
CBHW070333090426
42733CB00012B/2464